# Petrified Forest
## A STORY IN STONE

by Dr. Sidney Ash

Petrified Forest
Museum Association

Petrified Forest National Park, located in northeastern
Arizona, was established to protect multi-colored stone
trees and other plant and animal fossils; Native American
sites and petroglyphs; and portions of the Painted Desert.

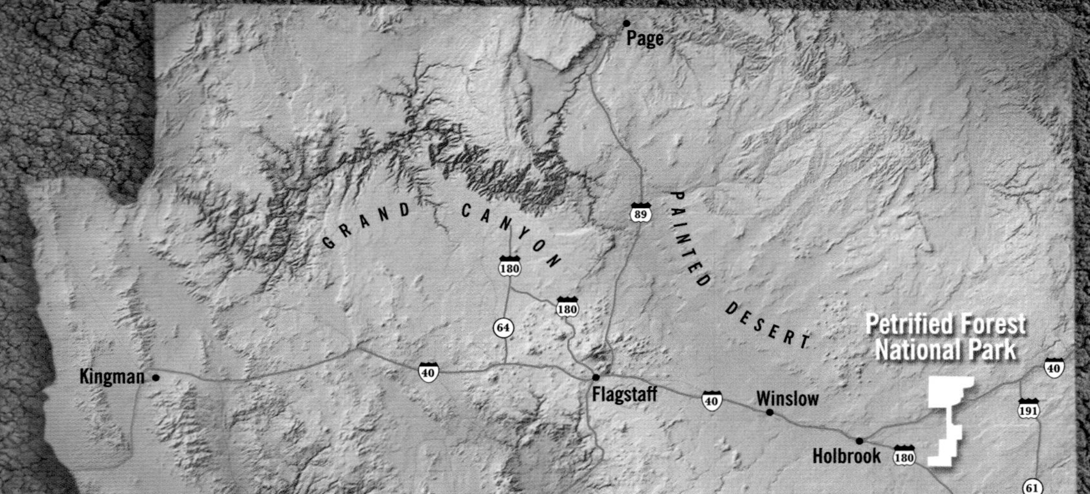

Page

GRAND CANYON

PAINTED DESERT

89

180

180

64

Petrified Forest
National Park

Kingman

40

40

Flagstaff

Winslow

40

191

Holbrook

180

61

17

Phoenix

10

8

10

Yuma

Tucson

19

10

# Contents

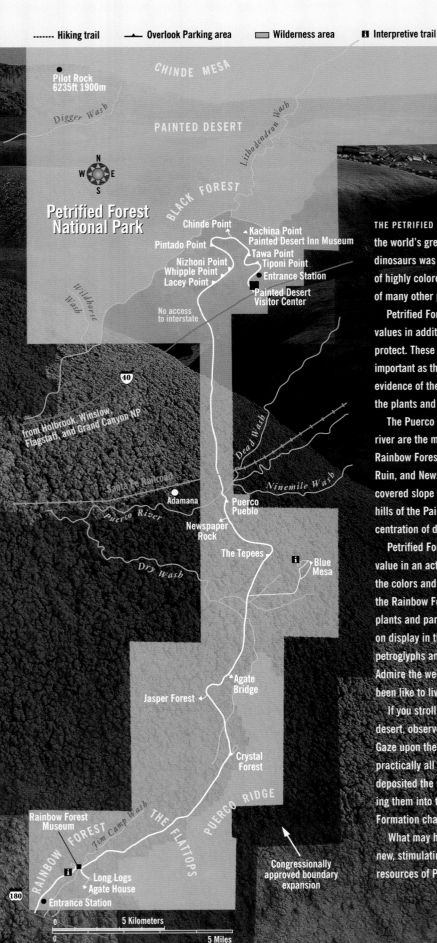

------ Hiking trail    ▲— Overlook Parking area    ▭ Wilderness area    ℹ️ Interpretive trail

**Petrified Forest National Park**

Pilot Rock
6235ft 1900m

Digger Wash

CHINDE MESA

PAINTED DESERT

Lithodendron Wash

BLACK FOREST

Chinde Point

Pintado Point

Kachina Point
Painted Desert Inn Museum

Tawa Point
Tiponi Point

Nizhoni Point
Whipple Point
Lacey Point

Entrance Station

Painted Desert
Visitor Center

Wildhorse Wash

No access
to interstate

40

from Holbrook, Winslow,
Flagstaff, and Grand Canyon NP

Dead Wash

Santa Fe Railroad

Ninemile Wash

Adamana

Puerco River

Puerco
Pueblo

Newspaper
Rock

Dry Wash

The Tepees

ℹ️ Blue
Mesa

Agate
Bridge

Jasper Forest

Crystal
Forest

PUERCO RIDGE

Congressionally
approved boundary
expansion

Rainbow Forest
Museum

Jim Camp Wash

THE FLATTOPS

RAINBOW FOREST

ℹ️

Long Logs

Agate House

180

Entrance Station

0    5 Kilometers

0    5 Miles

# INTRODUCTION

THE PETRIFIED FOREST is a land of quiet grandeur and vivid contrasts. It is also one of the world's greatest storehouses of knowledge about life on earth when the age of the dinosaurs was just beginning. In fact, what is probably the world's largest concentration of highly colored petrified wood occurs in the Petrified Forest together with the remains of many other plants and animals that lived here at that same time.

Petrified Forest National Park contains a wealth of scenic, scientific, and historical values in addition to the petrified wood that the original monument was designated to protect. These include many other types of fossils, both plant and animal, that are as important as the fossil wood, if not more so. Throughout the park there is also abundant evidence of the Native Americans who once lived here. An added dimension is given by the plants and animals that now live in the park.

The Puerco River naturally divides the park into two distinct sections. South of the river are the main concentrations of petrified wood at Jasper Forest, Crystal Forest, and Rainbow Forest. Here also are the Tepees, Blue Mesa, Agate Bridge, the Flattops, Puerco Ruin, and Newspaper Rock. North of the Puerco River is a broad, undulating sagebrush-covered slope that abruptly gives way along a steep, high cliff to the colorful but barren hills of the Painted Desert. Also found in this part of the park is a relatively small concentration of dark-colored petrified wood called the Black Forest.

Petrified Forest National Park offers an exercise in serendipity: the finding of greater value in an activity than expected. Examine pieces of petrified wood closely and enjoy the colors and patterns that make them unique. Study the logs and the fossil leaves in the Rainbow Forest Museum and imagine what they were like when they were living plants and part of an ancient forest. Look at the bones and teeth of the extinct animals on display in the park museums and visualize what these creatures looked like. View the petroglyphs and try to determine what the artist wanted to convey with these designs. Admire the well-built walls of the rooms at Puerco Ruin and think what it would have been like to live there when the pueblo was inhabited.

If you stroll away from the path at one of the viewpoints and into the quiet of the desert, observe the natural vegetation and some of the wildlife that inhabit the park. Gaze upon the intricately carved badlands in the Painted Desert and remember that practically all that you see here was produced by the action of water. Running water deposited the sediments that form the Chinle Formation, and running water is now eroding them into these strange forms. Finally, watch the variegated colors in the Chinle Formation change during a cloud-filled day.

What may have started as a reluctant break in a high-speed trip can become a totally new, stimulating, and rewarding experience for those who take the time to enjoy the resources of Petrified Forest National Park.

# Setting the Geologic Scene

**Opposite:** Weathering and the erosion action of water flowing over a bed of soft sandstone in the Chinle Formation have produced these unusual rounded forms.

**Top:** Broken fragments of petrified logs litter the surface of the ground in Rainbow Forest. The colorful bands in the hills are thought to be ancient soil horizons.

**Right:** A pedestal log on Blue Mesa. Originally the log was buried in a bed of sand and gravel on the bottom of an ancient stream channel. However, after many years passed, erosion began removing the sand and gravel and the log was once again exposed. In time, all the sediments from beneath the log will be removed and the log will tumble down the slope and disintegrate.

THE FAMOUS PETRIFIED FORESTS that are protected in Petrified Forest National Park occur in a colorfully banded sequence of rocks called the Chinle Formation, which is widely exposed in many parts of the southwestern United States. The rocks that form the Painted Desert are also included in the Chinle. This formation was deposited about 220 to 225 million years ago near the end of the Triassic period of the Mesozoic (middle life) era on still older rocks. These older rocks are not exposed in the Petrified Forest, but some of them are visible in surrounding areas and in Grand Canyon National Park and Canyon de Chelly National Monument. Only a few younger rocks are present in the Petrified Forest. They are assigned to the Bidahochi (Bid-ah-HO-chee) Formation of the Tertiary period of the Cenozoic (modern life) era and are thought to be four to eight million years old. Large exposures of the Bidahochi Formation also occur just north of the park and cover several parts of northeastern Arizona.

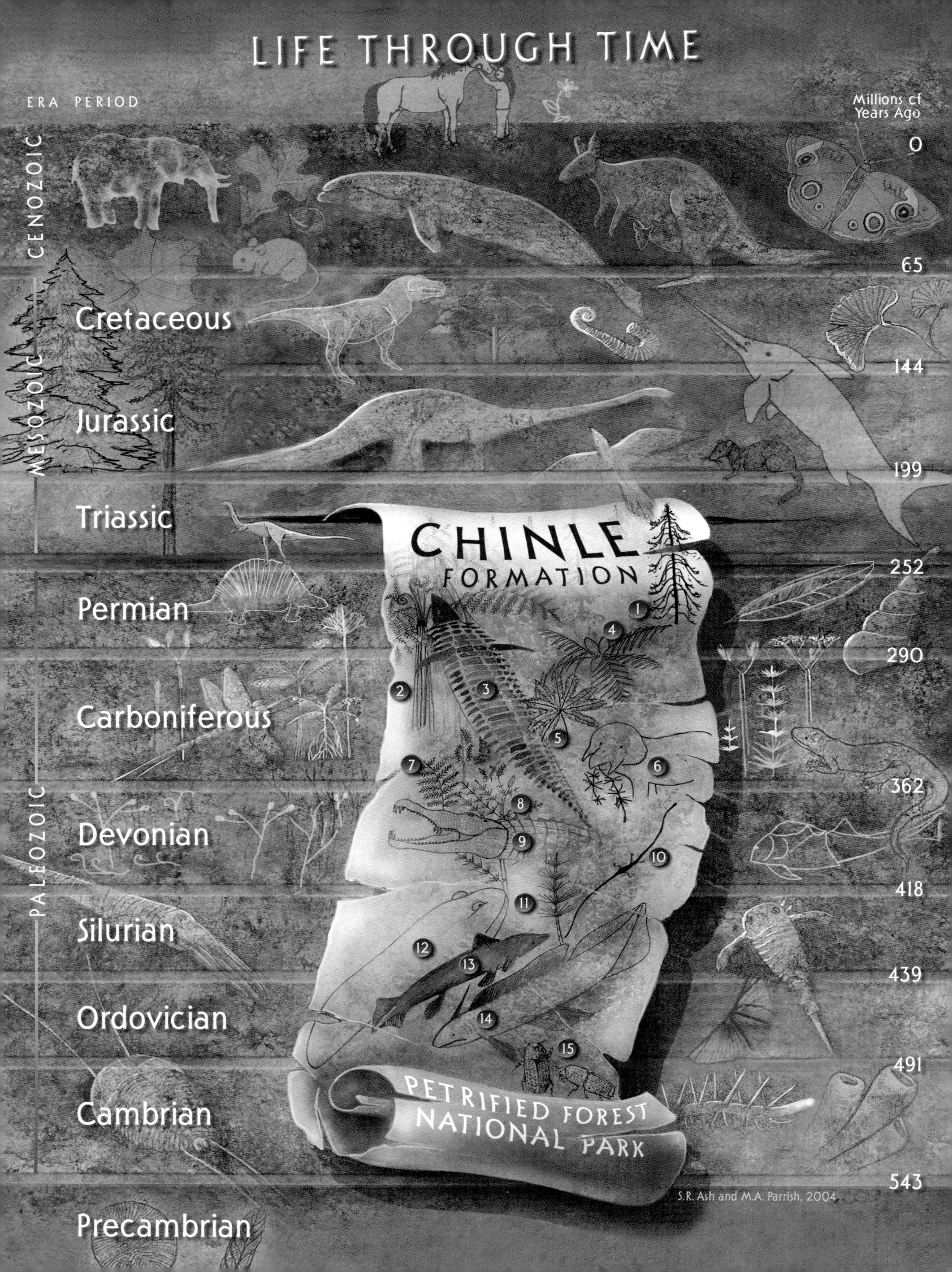

# LIFE THROUGH TIME

ERA  PERIOD

Millions of Years Ago

CENOZOIC

0

65

MESOZOIC

Cretaceous

144

Jurassic

199

Triassic

252

Permian

290

PALEOZOIC

Carboniferous

362

Devonian

418

Silurian

439

Ordovician

491

Cambrian

543

Precambrian

CHINLE FORMATION

PETRIFIED FOREST NATIONAL PARK

S.R. Ash and M.A. Parrish. 2004

**Right:** Typical view of the Chinle Formation on a stormy day in the Painted Desert. The light-colored layer on the top of the rounded hills in the foreground is the Black Forest bed, and the dark blocks on its surface are sections of petrified logs that have been exposed by erosion. As time passes and erosion continues, the hills will become smaller and smaller and all of the logs will eventually tumble down to the desert floor.

**Chinle Plants and Animals**
*(opposite)*

1. Conifer tree *Araucarioxylon*
2. Tree fern *Itopsidema*
3. Aetosaur *Desmatosuchus*
4. Cycad *Lyssoxylon*
5. Fern *Clathropteris*
6. Reptile *Placerias*
7. Fern *Wingatea*
8. Giant Horsetail *Neocalamites*
9. Phytosaur *Leptosuchus*
10. Lizard-like reptile *Tanystropheus*
11. Horsetail *Equisetites*
12. Metoposaur *Buettneria*
13. Coelacanth *Chinlea*
14. Prong-toothed shark *Xenacanthus*
15. Bark beetle

## The Chinle Formation

The Chinle Formation consists of a variety of sedimentary rock types. Most of the rocks in the Chinle are soft, fine-grained mudstone, siltstone, and claystone. But it also contains some beds of much harder and more coarsely-grained sandstone and conglomerate and near the top of the formation is a series of limestone beds. Most beds of rock in the Chinle do not extend over a great distance laterally but tend to thin and disappear or to blend into rock of a different texture.

In the vicinity of the Petrified Forest the Chinle Formation is about 800-feet-thick, although it is nearly twice as thick in western New Mexico. Within the Petrified Forest and the Painted Desert, as in many areas of the southwestern United States, the Chinle exhibits a striking range of pastel colors. These variations in color are the most noticeable characteristic of the formation and usually make it easily recognizable wherever it occurs.

The Painted Desert does in fact derive its name from the colorful rocks that are so characteristic of the Chinle Formation. Various combinations of minerals and other substances in the Chinle provide tones that seem to encompass all shades of the rainbow. For example, iron oxides in varying amounts are responsible for the wide range of red tones in the Painted Desert and elsewhere in this formation. Decayed plant and animal matter usually contribute the gray color found in the Chinle. The white coloring in the prominent but thin layer of rock in the Painted Desert north of Kachina Point is due to volcanic ash. This distinctive layer is incongruently called the Black Forest Bed because it contains the large concentration of black logs called the Black Forest.

In the Chinle Formation, the tone of colors can change quickly. What appears as a brilliant assortment of intense colors at one time may look dull and unimpressive at another. As a general rule, color is least intense at midday and most brilliant very early and very late in the day. Following a rain when the rocks are wet and the sky is clear, the colors are more vivid than when they are dry and dusty. On a partly cloudy day when the surface of the earth is a mosaic of light and shadow, the contrast between shaded and sunlit areas makes the latter appear even more brilliant.

When exposed to forces of erosion for a short time, the Chinle Formation usually develops into badlands. Sandstone and conglomerate resist erosion, forming cliffs and fostering the development of mesas (broad flat-topped hills) such as Blue Mesa and buttes (small flat-topped hills) like the Haystacks. When the protective layers of hard sandstone and conglomerate are removed, the softer beds of shale and mudstone erode much more rapidly and tend to produce sloping hillsides and narrow gullies. Consequently, the soft beds form conical hills and mounds instead of flat-topped features. In some cases, the running water also seeps into cracks in the soft sediment and forms small temporary caves that develop near the base of the hills. The scarcity of vegetation in the area accentuates the effect of rainfall and running water on the Chinle and thus accelerates the development of badlands.

Most of the sediments that make up the Chinle Formation were deposited by streams meandering northwestwardly across a broad plain of fairly low relief in northern Arizona and adjacent areas in Utah and New Mexico. An especially prominent example of one of these stream deposits in the central part of the park is the thick bed of sandstone and conglomerate on the top of Blue Mesa and the mesa that

contains Agate Bridge. Between the streams were marshes, swamps, lakes, and ponds. In places in the overbank areas soils developed on the dry land. These so-called overbank deposits are well exposed in the small hills called the Tepees in the central part of the park and adjacent areas. The abundance of freshwater limestone in the upper part of the Chinle in the northern part of the park suggests that there were extensive freshwater lakes in northern Arizona at the end of the Triassic.

It is unclear what happened in the Petrified Forest area after the Chinle Formation was deposited, because erosion has removed so much of the evidence. Presumably, periods of deposition and erosion occurred here at various times during the rest of the Mesozoic and possibly during the early part of the Cenozoic era. Probably, the sea even covered the area during the Cretaceous period near the end of the Mesozoic for marine strata of that age are present in nearby places. During the early Cenozoic, the region was deeply eroded for many years, but eventually, conditions changed again during the late Cenozoic, and another formation—the Bidahochi Formation—was deposited over the deeply eroded Chinle.

**Above:** A water-worn petrified log is highlighted by the sun on a cloudy day near Blue Mesa. **Left:** Pedestal log, the long-standing icon of the Petrified Forest, finally succumed to the forces of erosion and fell January 25, 2005. **Below:** A conical hill composed of relatively soft mudstone in the Chinle Formation. The interesting dendritic pattern on its surface was formed by running water from rain and melting snow that flowed down the hill.

## Bidahochi Formation

The Bidahochi Formation consists mostly of soft, light-colored sandstone, siltstone, and claystone and some hard beds of basalt, or lava. During the late Cenozoic, these sediments accumulated on the floor of a large, shallow lake that had formed in northeastern Arizona. At times, volcanic eruptions also occurred in the area and some of the lava flowed into the lake. Eventually, the lake dried up, and the lake sediments were covered with lava flows and volcanic ash. Then, the adjacent volcanoes erupted again. Additional sediments were deposited over the volcanic materials by streams and rivers. However, conditions changed again, and erosion then removed most of the Bidahochi in the Petrified Forest, although a small portion is still present in the northern part. The light-colored sandstone on top of Pilot Rock and below Tiponi Point, as well as the dark lava on Pilot Rock and along the rim of the Painted Desert from Pintado Point to Tawa Point, are assigned to the Bidahochi Formation.

## The Erosion Process

In the years since the deposition of the Bidahochi, erosion has cut deeply into that formation and even into the underlying Chinle Formation. As a consequence, large concentrations of petrified wood and other fossils have been exposed in the park and nearby areas. Most of the sediment that was removed did not travel far but was redeposited downstream in the broad valley of the Puerco River. Some of the eroded material, however, was swept into the Little Colorado River, through the Grand Canyon, and ultimately into the Gulf of California. Although water still flows along the same route, most of the sediment now accumulates behind Hoover Dam on the floor of Lake Mead. A small amount of the eroded material was not removed from the park and has accumulated on the floors of the depressions between the hills where it has become soil. Some of the more sandy sediment is preserved in sand dunes such as those found on the east side of the park road in the vicinity of the Tepees.

The erosion cycle continues, and each year a little more petrified wood and other fossils are exposed. Studies suggest that each year about one quarter of an inch of soil is removed from the steeper slopes in the park. Less than half that amount is removed from gentle slopes, and still less is eroded from level areas. Locally, the vagaries of wind and moving water may allow deposition for a short time, but the long-term trend is removal of more and more material.

**Above:** The palmate leaf of the fern *Clathropteris walkerii* was found in the Chinle Formation. Its descendants now live naturally in parts of Southeast Asia.
**Left:** The bands of tan-colored strata near the top of the view were deposited in a lake about 50 million years ago and are assigned to the Bidahochi Formation. The red mudstones below the Bidahochi Formation are assigned to the Chinle Formation.

Parrish '03

## Ancient Arizona During the Late Triassic

Scientists tell us that during the Late Triassic, America was several thousand miles southeast of its present location and much closer to the equator than it is now. As a result, ancient Arizona was then at about the latitude of Panama but at a position that is now in the middle of the Atlantic Ocean about halfway between South America and Africa. At that time, North America had just separated from western Africa and South America and had begun drifting northwestwardly toward its present location. Thus, much of the continent was then in the tropics.

In the Late Triassic, northeastern Arizona was a plain with rather low relief. South and southeast of the plain in what is now southern Arizona and New Mexico, there was a chain of mountains sometimes called the Mogollon Highlands. To the west, the sea was present in the region of modern-day southern California and western Nevada. Many streams that had

their headwaters in the Mogollon Highlands meandered northwestwardly across the plain on their way to the sea. These streams carried sediment from the highlands and deposited it in the stream channels and on floodplains. Between the streams were low hills, swamps, and small lakes. The climate was warm and moist, and the land was covered with many types of vegetation such as ferns, horsetails, conifers, and cycads (SIGH-cads—plants that superficially resemble palms but are not closely related to them).

Many types of fish, clams, snails, and crayfish abounded in the streams and lakes. Various species of insects were also present in the area, including beetles of several types and locust-like insects. A variety of amphibians, reptiles, and mammal-like reptiles lived on the ground and, in some cases, in nearby bodies of water. All of them competed with each other for food and space.

In addition to sediment, the streams that crossed the plain also carried logs from nearby areas to the south. When the banks of these streams were eroded, the trees that grew nearby fell into the moving water and were also transported northwardly toward the sea. As time passed, some of the logs became mired in mud and covered with sediment at the bottom of streams. In other locations, floodwaters carried logs out of the river channels and deposited them on adjacent floodplains. Seeds and leaves fell off the plants that lived in the area and accumulated on the ground or in shallow lakes. Animals died and their remains accumulated on the ground, on the floor of the shifting streams, and in the lakes. As the rivers deposited their loads of sediment, countless numbers of plant and animal remains were buried. With the passing of time, the Chinle Formation grew thicker, and more plant and animal remains were entombed in the growing deposit and were then fossilized.

## Fossilization

Although the fossilization process has been studied for many years, it is not completely understood by scientists. Usually when an organism dies, its remains decay rapidly or are eaten by scavengers. As a result, all visible traces of dead organisms disappear completely within a relatively short time. In some cases, such as in the Petrified Forest, these processes did not always take place, and parts of many organisms were fossilized. However, even if fossils do form, they may be destroyed later by natural forces or remain buried and unknown to scientists. But in unusual situations, as in the Petrified Forest, the right conditions have prevailed, and not only were many fossils formed but many have also been exposed—and are still being exposed—by erosion.

The rate of fossilization depends largely upon the environment in which the potential fossil is buried. Temperature, moisture, oxygen supply, depth of burial, elements present in the surrounding sediments, and perhaps other factors have an important effect on what happens to the organic matter in a potential fossil. The rate of fossilization varies greatly according to circumstances. In the Petrified Forest, however, it appears that fossilization of the logs must have occurred rather rapidly because most of them are nearly round in cross section, much as they were in life. In other words, they were fossilized before the overlying layers of sediment became so heavy that the logs were crushed and flattened.

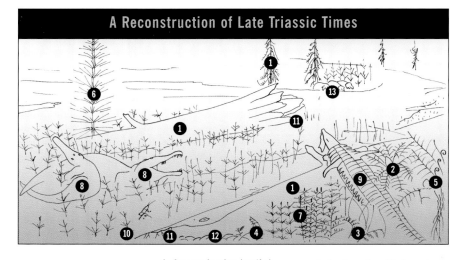

### A Reconstruction of Late Triassic Times

1. *Araucarioxylon* (conifer)
2. *Aricycas* (cycad)
3. *Cynepteris* (fern)
4. *Wingatea* (fern)
5. *Itopsidema* (tree fern)
6. *Neocalamites* (horsetail)
7. *Equisetum* (horsetail)
8. *Leptosuchus* (Phytosaur)
9. *Desmatosuchus* (Aetosaur)
10. *Enoploclytia* (crayfish)
11. Beetles with burrows
12. *Selaginella* (clubmoss)
13. *Placerias* (reptile)

Several types of fossilization are represented in the Petrified Forest. The main type of fossilization is petrification, where wood and bones are turned to stone. Two types of petrification are found in the park. In the first type, all or practically all of the organic matter in potential fossils was replaced by mineral matter. The resulting fossil has the external form of the object but little or none of the internal cellular structure is still present. In the Petrified Forest most of the logs have been replaced at least in part by mineral matter, especially varieties of quartz, and they now contain little, if any, of the original organic matter. The colorful logs in the Rainbow Forest in the southern part of the park are good examples of fossils that have been preserved by replacement.

In the second type of petrification the cells and other spaces in the potential fossil are filled with mineral matter, but much of the original organic matter remains unchanged. In this type of petrification, or permineralization, much of the cellular detail in the fossil is preserved and can be observed with a microscope. Only a small proportion of the logs and stumps

**Opposite:** Short sections of light-colored petrified logs rest on somber beds of the Chinle Formation in the Blue Mesa area of the park. Several logs are visible on the mesa top in the middle. **Top right:** These sections of colorful petrified wood are slowly sliding down the side of a hill of gray mudstone in the Chinle Formation. **Right:** A researcher careful looks for fossil plant remains in the gray mudstone of the Chinle Formation near the Tepees. **Bottom:** Hoodoos in Crystal Forest. Such strange-looking columns are formed by differential erosion of beds alternating between hard and soft rock.

in the park have been permineralized, whereas most of the bones have been preserved in this manner. The logs in the Black Forest in the northern part of the park are generally black because they have been permineralized. Interestingly, parts of some logs in the park have been totally replaced by mineral matter and other parts of the same logs are permineralized, so it is possible to find specimens containing both types of presertion.

Petrified wood and bone are surprisingly heavy and hard. Quartz is relatively heavy and hard, and an object such as a bone or a log that has been petrified by that mineral is several times heavier and harder than the original material. A cubic foot of petrified wood weighs about 168 pounds and has a hardness of about 7 on a scale of

hardness from 1 to 10. In contrast, the wood of living trees only weighs a few pounds per cubic foot and has a hardness of 1 to 2 on the same scale.

Typically, the leaves, seeds, cones, pollen grains, spores, and small stems, together with animal remains from fish and insects were preserved as compression fossils. This type of preservation forms when a potential fossil is buried in sediment and then flattened by the weight of the overlying rock so that only a thin film of carbonaceous material is left in the rock. When the enclosing rock is split, the fossil will look like a layer of black paint on the freshly broken surface of the rock. Such fossils may show great detail and are often very valuable in helping scientists reconstruct and understand ancient plants and animals.

In the Petrified Forest, the sediments deposited by Upper Triassic rivers were saturated with water, which decreased the rate of decay of the plant and animal remains they entombed. The same water that slowed the decay of the logs and bones had earlier filtered through sediments rich in the element silicon. As the silicon-rich water slowly percolated through the logs and bones, the silicon came out of solution and combined with oxygen to form minute crystals of quartz within the spaces in the tissues and formed permineralized fossils. In other cases, it even replaced the organic matter forming replacement fossils.

A majority of the fossil logs here are solidly petrified, and all the tissue has been filled or replaced by quartz. However, inside hollow logs or in cracks in otherwise solid logs the growth of quartz crystals was not restricted by cell structure or adjoining crystals. As a consequence, cavities within the wood are sometimes lined or even filled with large crystals of amethyst, rose quartz, smoky quartz, and rock crystal quartz. Examples of logs that contain such crystal-lined cavities are often found in the Crystal Forest.

The water that provided the silica for petrification also contained other elements that were incorporated

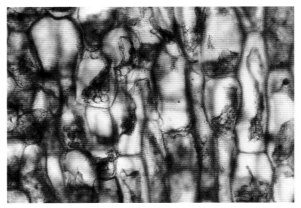

into the wood and were responsible for the variety of colors in the fossils. Iron, probably the most common element incorporated in the developing fossils after silicon, produced various shades of red, yellow, brown, and even blue. Cobalt and chromium, rarely included, provided blue and green coloring. Carbon and sometimes manganese added black. Interestingly, manganese was also responsible for some of the pink coloring. Most of the wood contains a variety of colors and tones that are composed of just a few primary colors. Blends of yellow, red, black, blue, and white provide an amazing range of hues.

**Above:** The desert floor in this part of the park is covered with a dense layer of fragments of petrified wood that vary greatly in size. The hill in the background is composed mostly of mudstone and contains a thin discontinuous bed of sandstone that forms a low cliff and overhang in places on the sides of the hill. **Left:** A thin section of permineralized wood (enlarged about 100 times) shows well-preserved cells and possible cellular contents.

## Petrified Wood and Its Sources
*by Paul Sell DoBell II*
Executive Director, Petrified Forest Museum Association

Petrified wood is hard enough to score glass, but it is comprised primarily of silica, or quartz. This form of fossilization has been repeated periodically throughout earth's history, leaving deposits of petrified wood all over the world. The types, composition, and look of these deposits vary greatly, from fairly colorless to brightly colored, multicolored to uniform coloration, and recognizable as petrified wood to what would appear to be nothing more than a rock or piece of jasper. The differences are due to the type of trees being petrified, environmental conditions, trace minerals, and other elements present at the time when the trees were buried and the petrification process began.

Indeed, petrified wood is not only represented in every state of the United States of America, but it is also found scattered around the globe. Commercial use of petrified wood began in the Southwest with the ancestors of the modern Native Americans, who used and shaped this material into various tools, including sharp-edged cutting instruments, spears, and arrowheads. These durable pieces were traded, perhaps in exchange for pottery, seashells, furs, and other items. Petrified wood was also used as a building material due to its abundance in and around the park.

The commercial use of petrified wood as a souvenir coincided with increased visitation to the Four Corners area, sparking concerns that ongoing losses would eliminate the attraction to the area. In response to these concerns, the National Park Service, which maintains the Petrified Forest National Park, was entrusted with the protection and preservation of less than 10% of the Chinle formation, the formation in which petrified wood is found. This management leaves the balance of preservation on both public and private land. Today, all of the petrified wood that is acquired for resale comes from private land, allowing our public park to be home to one of the best-preserved examples of the Chinle formation.

Despite the availability of commercially sold petrified wood and the ongoing efforts of the National Park Service to protect this small refuge, there are still those that would chose to remove a small piece of petrified wood from within Petrified Forest National Park. This act forever reduces the park's ability to remain a pristine preserve for future generations. With visitation at the park ranging between 500,000 to 1,000,000 visitors a year, that "one" piece can add up quickly and destroy this unique outdoor museum. This is not only a crime, but it is also an unnecessary price that will be paid by future generations who are not able to share this experience.

**Left:** Frank Albert DoBell at DoBell Curio circa 1950 with young visitors to the area.

# Life of an Ancient Landscape

FOSSILS FOUND IN THE PETRIFIED FOREST indicate that a surprising variety of plants and animals lived in the area during the Late Triassic when the Chinle Formation was being deposited. These fossils, which represent many elements of a 225 million-year-old ecosystem, include not only petrified wood but also leaves, cones, seeds, and other plant parts. In addition, fossilized remains of clams, snails, clam shrimp, horseshoe crabs, crayfish, insects, fish, amphibians, and reptiles, including dinosaurs, are also found in the park. Although some of the plants and animals would have resembled modern species, many would have been totally unfamiliar and even quite bizarre. In addition, several would have looked like giant copies of certain living forms.

Our knowledge of the ancient life of the Petrified Forest is the product of the work of many scientists who have spent years digging up fossils and studying them in the laboratory. Their conclusions are based not only on fossils found here but also on comparisons with fossils found elsewhere in the world and with living plants and animals.

The size, form, and structures of plant fossils tell us much about the size and growth habits of the original plants. Some structures on the leaves can tell us about the climate in which the plant lived.

Similarly, fossilized animal remains can provide us with much information about living animals. For example, we can deduce the dimensions and some of the habits of extinct creatures from fossilized bones and teeth. The size and shape of leg bones can reveal much about how the animals moved—whether they sprawled in swamps or ran about on land on two or four legs. Teeth are very informative because they give clues about the diet of the creatures and their size as well. If the teeth are suited only for tearing flesh, the owner was carnivorous and preyed on other animals. Very different types of teeth are required by herbivores, which bite and chew vegetation. Intermediate types of teeth indicate the varied diet of omnivorous creatures, who, like many of us, enjoyed a little salad with their steak.

## Plants

The most obvious and common plant fossil found in the Chinle Formation is petrified wood. However, as interesting and attractive as the wood may be, it is not as scientifically important as the other plant fossils that occur in the formation. These less obvious fossils tell us much more about the variety and types of plants that once lived here and the environment they lived in. They include small compressed stems, leaves, seeds, and cones and large numbers of the microscopic spores and pollen grains produced by ancient plants.

Of the 200 species of plants identified from the Chinle only 9 are based on petrified wood; another 80 on compressed leaves, stems, seeds, and cones; and the remainder on spores, pollen grains, and other small plant parts. Many of the species were originally described from material collected in the park but have since been found elsewhere in the Southwest. A few have even been reported from Upper Triassic rocks in eastern North America. All of the plant species that flourished here during the Upper Triassic are extinct, but the modern descendants of several now live naturally in humid tropical regions of the world.

Most major plant groups are represented in the Chinle Formation, the flowering plants being the principal exception. Horsetails, or scouring rushes, are a primitive group of plants that occur commonly in the Chinle Formation at many localities. The fossil and living members in this group have straight, slender, hollow stems that are jointed. The common name of these plants derives from the fact that people have thought that the plants looked like the tails of horses. Pioneers reportedly used the stems to scour their pots and pans, which explains the origin of the other common name.

Stems of living horsetails rarely grow more than 6 to 12 feet tall or more than one half inch in diameter. In the Petrified Forest, however, the stems of some ancient representatives of the group, called *Neocalamites*, have a diameter of 14 to 16 inches and represent plants that were probably 20 to 30 feet tall. Stems of another horsetail found in the park, *Equisetites*, are only 1 to 1 1/2 inches in diameter, and these plants were probably only 10 to 15 feet tall. Living horsetails now grow naturally in many parts of the world where there are dependable sources of water, but the largest (up to 12 feet tall) grow in moist tropical parts of the world.

One of the most abundant and varied groups of fossilized plants known from the park is the fern. This group is represented here by the fronds, stems, and spores of perhaps a dozen species.

**Top left:** A fragment of the leaf of the fern *Cynepteris lasiophora* from the Chinle Formation.
**Top right:** A thin section of a small piece of *Araucarioxylon arizonicum* wood that has been permineralized so that the cell structure is preserved.
**Left:** Ghosts of cell walls are visible in a small piece of colorful *Araucarioxylon arizonicum* wood that has been nearly completely replaced by quartz. The red color comes from iron minerals mixed into the quartz.

**Right:** An artist's impression of an ancient Triassic floodplain. **Below:** This microscopic view shows three pollen grains that were probably produced by one of the conifers that lived in this area during the Late Triassic. **Middle Right:** Several specimens of the palmate leaf of *Phlebopteris smithii* from the Chinle Formation. The descendants of this fern now live naturally in parts of Southeast Asia. **Bottom Right:** A small fragment (enlarged about 1,000 times) of unaltered cuticle from the leaf of the strange gymnosperm *Dinophyton spinosus*. Unaltered bits of cuticle like this are commonly found in the Chinle Formation in the Petrified Forest.

The fronds form black compressions and are often found complete and so well preserved that it is possible to study details of their epidermis and other fine structures through a microscope. Some ferns like *Wingatea plumosa* had delicate and highly dissected pinnate (feather-like) leaves. Others, such as *Phlebopteris smithii* and *Clathropteris walkerii*, had palmate leaves with leaflets radiating out from a common center, similar to the fingers on our hands. These two species are of particular interest because their closest living relatives are now found living naturally in the humid tropics of Southeast Asia.

The trunk of a tree fern, *Itopsidema vancleavei*, has been found in the park. Whereas the leaves of most ferns grow directly from an underground stem, or rhizome (RYE-zoam), the leaves of this plant grew out of the top of a thick upright aerial stem or trunk and formed a large canopy. The lower part of the stem was sheathed with a mat of small roots that more or less buttressed the stem, enabling it to stand upright and the upper part was covered by the broken bases of old leaves. The *Itopsidema vancleavei* plant may have been 6 or more feet tall.

Superficially, the plant would have looked like a miniature palm, but this interesting plant was actually a distant relative of some of the modern tree ferns that now grow naturally in the humid tropics in many parts of the world.

Fossilized remains of many types of seed plants occur abundantly in the Petrified Forest and elsewhere in the Chinle Formation in the Southwest. Many of the fossils found here represent organisms that are related to living groups of plants, but several appear to represent groups that are now extinct.

The conifers are particularly well represented in the Petrified Forest, for most of the logs here are the remains of such cone-bearing trees. The majority of these trees were very tall. On average, the logs are about 80 to 100 feet long and 3 to 4 feet in diameter, but some range up to about 130 feet in length and 10 feet in diameter at the base. Typically, the trunks are battered and worn, without bark, limbs, or roots, but stumps of small limbs and roots are present on some of them. The condition of the logs indicates that most were carried some distance by streams before being buried and fossilized. While the logs were being transported, the limbs and roots were broken off, the bark removed, and the trunks generally abraded and battered.

At several places in the park a few upright tree stumps 2 to 3 feet in diameter and only a few feet tall have been found in the position of growth with their roots extending downward into the ground. These stumps demonstrate that there were at least small groves of large trees growing here when the Chinle was being deposited.

Most of the wood in the park is assigned to Araucarioxylon arizonicum, because it was originally thought to have come from trees that were early members of the Araucaria family, which now lives naturally in parts of the southern hemisphere. Recent studies, however, indicate that this idea is not true and that the nearest living relatives are actually uncertain. Nevertheless, it is obvious that the wood came from stately trees that must have dominated the Late Triassic landscape in this area. It is estimated that the

tallest of these trees were as much as 180 feet tall and nearly 10 feet in diameter at the base. The trunk called "Old Faithful" is an example of one of the tallest of these trees and is estimated to have contained enough lumber to make a wood frame house containing about 2000 square feet of floor space.

Except for the limbs being irregularly arranged on the trunk, the living *Araucarioxylon arizonicum* tree would not have looked very different from most large conifers that have a single main trunk. Its root system consisted of a thick tap root surrounded by a ring of thick steeply inclined lateral roots, a type of root system that was well designed for trees growing in thick soft water-soaked soils near streams and other bodies of water. Unfortunately, the leaves, cones, and seeds of the *Araucarioxylon arizonicum* tree are not known, but the recent discovery of a bark-clad branch in the Painted Desert gives us valuable insight into that important part of the plant. The fossil shows that the bark was relatively thin and comparable to the scale bark on many living conifers. Since fossil bark is rarely found, this branch must have been buried and fossilized shortly after it broke off of the parent trunk and before it was transported any significant distance.

Two other types of wood, *Woodworthia* and *Schilderia*, occur in small quantities in the Black Forest in the northern part of the park. The wood of these types tends to be more subdued in coloring than *Araucarioxylon*. Also, both of these trees were smaller than the *Araucarioxylon arizonicum* trees.

**Top left:** The stump of an *Araucarioxylon arizonicum* tree still standing in the position of growth in the Painted Desert section of Petrified Forest National Park. Weathering has rounded the top of the stump somewhat since it was exposed by erosion.

**Above:** A bark-clad branch of the *Araucarioxylon arizonicum* tree found in the Chinle Formation in the Black Forest. It is very unusual for the bark of a tree to ever be preserved, because it usually falls off very soon after a tree dies.

**Opposite:** A hillside covered with fragments of petrified wood of various sizes.

**Below:** Somber beds of mudstone in the Chinle Formation are exposed in conical hills in the central part of the Petrified Forest.

The *Schilderia* trees were the larger of the two, with trunks that were up to nearly 3 feet in diameter and nearly 120 feet in length. In comparison, the trunks of the *Woodworthia* trees were somewhat smaller, only about 2 1/2 feet in diameter and the living trees were only about 100 feet tall.

Leafy twigs, cones, seeds, and pollen grains from several species of conifers occur at a few places in the Petrified Forest. The leaves are so well preserved that it is often possible to see their cell structure and the microscopic spines and hairs that grew on them. Most of the twigs that have been found are small and broken, suggesting that they, like most of the petrified logs, were transported some distance by streams from where they grew to where they were buried and fossilized.

Another plant found here that is related to a living form is the cycad *Charmorgia dijollii*. This plant had a short, globular stem about 12 inches tall and 10 inches in diameter. The exterior of the stem was covered with broken leaf bases, and the top had a crown of coarse leaves of some unknown type. A large colorful cone would have been present on the very top of the stem. A second and different type of cycad stem called *Lyssoxylon grigsbyi* has also been found in the park. It

had a 3- to 4-foot-tall columnar stem with a rough exterior covered with broken leaf bases. The plant would have had a crown of coarse leaves of some type. These two plants are closely related to cycads now naturally inhabiting the tropical parts of Australia, South America, and South Africa. Rather large pinnate leaves of a cycad occur at one locality in the park and are called *Aricycas paulae*. They too are similar to the leaves of certain living cycads and may have been borne by *Charmorgia dijollii* or a similar plant.

The leaves of a plant that was similar to a cycad are very abundant in the park. They come from the Bennettitales, an extinct group of plants that may be distantly related to the cycads. The leaves, called *Zamites powellii*, have a broad stem with a row of stiff, oblong leaflets on each side. This leaf is one of the most common in the entire Chinle Formation. It is not certain what the stem of the parent plant looked like, but the chances are that it had a columnar stem somewhat like *Lyssoxylon*.

**Top**: A polished cross section of a large trunk of the *Araucarioxylon arizonicum* tree. The red colors in the wood are a result of small amounts of iron minerals mixed with the mineral quartz, which is normally colorless. **Bottom:** A specimen of the bennettitalean leaf *Zamites powellii*. The stiff leaflets that occur on each side of the stem are clearly visible.
**Opposite:** Sections of the fossilized trunk of an *Araucarioxylon arizonicum* tree have fallen down a gully on the side of a mesa in the central part of the park.

2 cm

A number of plant fossils that are difficult to classify occur in the Chinle Formation. One of them is called *Dinophyton spinosus*, a name which means "terrible spiny plant." It is represented by leafy twigs that have long, narrow, pointed leaves and seed-bearing structures that have four linear wings. All of the surfaces of this plant were covered with tiny, spine-like structures. These structures were the source of its name, because the plant would have felt terrible to the touch. Another plant of uncertain relationship also has winged seeds of a different sort. This plant, called *Dechellyia gormanii*, had a pinnate leaf that looked something like *Zamites powellii*, but the *Dechellyia*'s leaflets were pointed, and the plant had single-winged seeds that were borne on short side stems at the base of the leaf.

Amber, the fossilized resin of plants, occurs at several localities in the park. Although amber is prized for jewelry, the pieces found here are quite small and fragmentary. The origin of the material is uncertain, but a specimen of wood from the *Araucarioxylon arizonicum* tree has been found outside of the park that has amber in it suggesting that at least some of the amber in the park could have come from the same tree.

A small amount of charcoal has been identified in the park showing that wildfires did occur here, at least occasionally during the Late Triassic. But since the charcoal is rare, it appears that wildfires were not very extensive, and as a result, did not disrupt the Chinle biota to a very high degree. The wildfires that did occur probably were caused by lightning, just as they are in tropical environments today.

**Left:** Large sections of petrified wood and many smaller fragments litter the ground surface in this area. **Top:** A leafy twig of the strange gymnosperm *Dinophyton spinosus* that was exposed when a small piece of the Chinle Formation was broken in half. **Above:** A hypothetical scene in the area the Petrified Forest of a bolt of lightening hitting the ground during the time the Chinle Formation was being deposited.

## Plants vs. Insects in the Petrified Forest

Just as a constant battle is taking place in modern forests between plants and insects, a similar battle was fought in the ancient forest that once existed in the Petrified Forest region during the Late Triassic period. Evidence consists of damaged plant fossils and a few insect fossils. The plants survived the attacks in most cases, but it is possible that some died. In other cases, the insects merely attacked plants that were already dead. Like some modern insects, such as bark beetles, the ancient insects infected the plants they attacked causing the plants to die. Like today, the insects occupied various niches in the Triassic food pyramid. Some helped break down plant and animal matter. They provided nourishment for small amphibians and reptiles. Some of the insects probably made sounds, especially those in the order that includes modern grasshoppers with sound producing and perceiving organs.

We do not know how common insects actually were in Petrified Forest National Park and vicinity during the Late Triassic. In the world today, they are the most extensive group of organisms within the animal kingdom. It is possible that they were just as common during the Late Triassic. In order to determine what insects were responsible for the damaged plant fossils, scientists must compare the damage in the fossils to that produced in living plants by modern insects. The diversity of damage found on plant fossils indicates that a large variety of insects were present. That information, combined with evidence offered by the insect fossils themselves, indicates that representatives of the beetle, fly, grasshopper, and dragonfly orders were present. The beetles may have been the most abundant, because most of the damage resembles that caused by modern beetles. One group of insects commonly found in many modern forests that might be expected here are termites. However, that group did not evolve until nearly 100 million years after the trees here died and were buried.

**Detail and Above:** Borings formed by ancient beetles just after the tree died. Some modern beetles form very similar borings.

**Left:** An artist's reconstruction of a prehistoric beetle passing through a tunnel bored into an ancient tree. **Background:** The fern leaf *Clathropteris walkerii*.

Leaves of several species of fossil ferns show evidence of attack by various types of insects. This evidence includes several forms of grazing marks. Large chunks along the margins of leaves were removed by one type of insect. In some cases, only the upper surface of the leaf was removed, exposing the flesh underneath for attack by other insects. In the third type of damage, insects ate holes all the way through the leaves. The presence of callous tissue along the edges of the incisions indicates that the leaves were alive when attacked and that all of them survived at least long enough to heal the wounds.

Many of the logs exposed in the park show various evidence of insect attack. The most common evidence consists of channels and channel fillings on the exterior of the trunks, which were formed between the wood and bark of the tree. In some specimens the channels completely encircle or girdle the trunks. It is possible that the trees died as a result of this damage. These structures closely resemble features formed on modern tress by living bark beetles. Some logs contain borings of different sizes, orientation, and distribution. The smaller borings are comparable to tunnels formed by modern powder-post beetles.

# Animals

Although they are generally delicate, the remains of invertebrate animals are found at a number of localities in the park. They include concentrations of freshwater clam and snail shells of several types. Shells of clam shrimp are abundant in some parts of the park, and trails made by a horseshoe crab have been found near Newspaper Rock. Compressions of beetles and cockroaches have been found in the same area. Furthermore, some of the petrified wood in the park shows evidence of having been attacked by bark beetles and several types of wood-boring insects, and some of the leaves had been nibbled on by insects.

Teeth, scales, and bones of many types of extinct freshwater fish have been found in the Chinle Formation. *Semionotus* was a small fish 3 to 5 inches long with heavily armored scales and teeth that indicate that it was a plant eater. *Arganodus* was a fish closely related to the modern lungfish that lives in small streams and ponds in parts of Australia, South Africa, and South America. When the streams and ponds begin to dry up, some lungfish survive by burrowing into muddy sediments, but the Chinle forms of fish did not.

**Top Right:** A Lungfish floats lifeless in the water above a pair of hungry prong-toothed sharks, as featured in the PFMA publication *Dawn of the Dinosaurs*. **Above:** A prong-toothed shark swims through a maze of giant horsetail trunks. This primitive shark was a slender, long-bodied fish that became extinct at the end of the Triassic period.

The remains of two kinds of sharks have been found in the area. *Lonchidion* was one of them. It was only about 9 inches long and had teeth, suggesting that it lived on small clams and clam shrimp. Another shark, *Xenocanthus*, may have been as long as 3 feet and probably fed on smaller fish, small aquatic reptiles, and amphibians.

*Chinlea* occupied the top of the food pyramid among the fish in the Chinle Formation. Most specimens are less than 2 feet long. Recent discoveries in the park indicate that this fish did reach a length of 5 feet, with a probable weight in excess of 150 pounds. *Chinlea* had large sharp teeth and would have been a formidable adversary.

Of the several four-legged animals present here in the Late Triassic some would have appeared vaguely familiar to us. Only amphibian and reptile fossils have been found, but it seems quite possible that the remains of early mammals will someday be discovered here as well. Some of the Triassic creatures resembled modern alligators and salamanders, but many others would appear very strange.

*Buettneria* is one of the common amphibians found in the park. It looked somewhat like a large salamander and was one of a primitive group of large amphibians that had been dominant during the Late Paleozoic. Most of this group failed to adapt to changing conditions and became extinct. *Buettneria* was one of the last of them. It had short, weak legs, a large, heavy body, and a big head. The amphibian was about 10 feet long and probably weighed about 1,000 pounds. This animal could not support itself on dry land, so it must have sprawled in the water and mud. Restricted to rivers, lakes, and swamps, where it probably fed on fish and other small animals, it was well adapted to the wet habitat and was apparently very common. Large concentrations of this amphibian are occasionally found. These concentrations presumably represent individuals that had gathered in water holes during dry periods but became trapped there and died when the water holes dried up.

Fossil remains of several groups of reptiles occur in the Chinle Formation. The most abundant are the large crocodile-like phytosaurs (FI-to-sors), which were also the dominant reptiles during most of Late Triassic time. Those found in the park have been assigned to the genera *Leptosuchus* and *Pseudopalatus*.

On average, they were about 17 feet long, but the remains of a giant that measured 30 feet long have been found. The front of the skull and the lower jaw of *Leptosuchus* formed a long, narrow snout. The jaws were set with numerous sharp, conical teeth, indicating that it preyed upon fish and animals living near water. The body and the tail were covered by heavy, bony plates, pieces of which are very commonly found in the park. This armor plating would have helped protect them from predators. The nostrils were located on a dome between and in front of the eyes, an adaptation that permitted the reptile to remain submerged for long periods of time while seeking prey.

Phytosaurs must have been efficient predators, because they could move about on dry land on their short, stubby legs and also stalk prey while submerged. Capable of moving from a pool to dry land, they were better adapted to changing environmental conditions than *Buettneria* and thus survived longer.

Remains of somewhat similar but different reptiles are commonly found in the park. These are the

aetosaurs, which like the phytosaurs were covered with heavy, bony plates. In addition, they had large spines on the sides and would have looked somewhat like armored crocodiles. They had long pig-like snouts and even though they may have looked dangerous, the snout and the teeth indicate that these curious reptiles probably ate insects and plants. The aetosaurs in the park averaged about 12 feet in length and probably weighed up to 1,000 pounds. Examples of aetosaurs found in the park include *Typothorax, Desmatosuchus, Stagonolepis,* and *Paratypothorax.*

Some people think of all prehistoric reptiles as dinosaurs, but the term "dinosaur" actually refers to a specific group of Mesozoic reptiles. One of the earliest-known dinosaurs in this region was *Coelophysis.* Compared to the better-known giants that evolved later, *Coelophysis* seems almost puny. It was only about 8 feet long and weighed about 50 pounds. At a much later time, some gigantic dinosaurs reached a length of 80 feet and a weight of 50 tons. *Coelophysis* had a long narrow tail and a long neck with a small head at the end that contained a mouth full of sharp, conical teeth. Its hind limbs were large and well developed, whereas the fore limbs were small, indicating that this dinosaur was bipedal.

**Top:** Shown are the compressed remains of a crayfish that once lived in the ancient streams and ponds of this area when it was swampy. This fossil closely resembles certain living crayfish.
**Bottom:** *Coelophysis* wading in a shallow Triassic pool inhabited by period residents: baby phytosaur, crayfish, bi-valve clams, and Triassic-era fish.

**Right:** An artist's illustration depicting an encounter between a *Postosuchus* and an aetosaur by a Triassic stream or floodplain edge.

**Bottom left:** An artist's reconstruction of a phytosaur when the Chinle Formation was being deposited.

**Bottom right:** A nearly complete well-preserved skull of a phytosaur.

**Pages 28-29:** During seasonal storms at Blue Mesa, torrents of water move swiftly across the ground, picking up vast quantities of sediment to carry toward the sea. As this occurs, the soft mudstone in the Chinle Formation erodes deeply and rapidly, exposing more and more petrified wood. At the same time, some of the support beneath the pedestal logs is washed away, accelerating their eventual destruction.

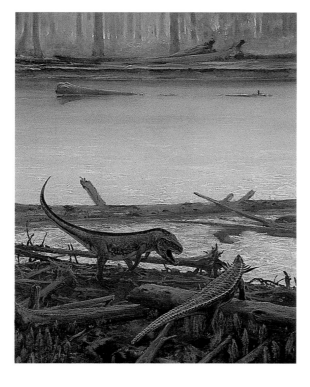

These characteristics suggest that *Coelophysis* was probably an active, vicious predator. Most of the known *Coelophysis* fossils were found in northern New Mexico many years ago, but recently, somewhat similar fossils were also found in the Petrified Forest.

The remains of a primitive dinosaur have been found in the park. *Chindesaurus* was built like *Coelophysis* but was probably somewhat larger and heavier. It too had sharp teeth indicating it was carnivorous. *Chindesaurus* had unusually long legs indicating that it could have been a fast runner allowing it to overtake and capture prey.

Recently, several skeletons of another reptile have been discovered in the park. *Revueltosaurus callenderi* was originally considered to be a plant-eating dinosaur based upon its teeth, which are commonly-found fossils in the Painted Desert. However, discovery of the rest of the skeleton has shown that this animal is not a dinosaur, but it is more closely related to a crocodile. This find provides the first documentation of a previously unknown group of herbivorous, crocodile-like reptiles present in the Late Triassic.

Remains of several other types of reptiles have been found in the Petrified Forest and in nearby exposures of the Chinle Formation. They include distant relatives of lizards that possessed extremely long, giraffe-like necks and lived in swamps and ponds. Another strange-looking animal was the rhinoceros-sized mammal-like reptile *Placerias*. Although this animal had a large, bulky body and probably weighed as much as 2 tons, it was herbivorous. It did not have teeth but had a horny bird-like beak and two strong forward pointing tusks, which probably were used to pull up roots and tubers and other plant parts for food. The mammal-like reptiles like *Placerias* were very significant in the history of life, because the mammals evolved from the group during the Triassic. However, shortly after the Triassic, the mammal-like reptiles became extinct.

The Late Triassic was a time of great changes. For some organisms like the phytosaurs, it was their last appearance. For others such as the dinosaurs, it was just the beginning of their domination of the land for nearly 150 million years. This was also a time when the plants were rapidly evolving and the land flora was beginning to appear more modern. Some of the plants, such as *Dinophyton* and *Dechellyia* apparently died out in the Triassic without leaving any direct descendants, whereas the ferns and cycads became more common as time passed.

# Humans in the Petrified Forest

THE PETRIFIED FOREST was discovered thousands of years ago by the ancestors of today's Native Americans and was inhabited by groups of them for varying lengths of time. More than 650 of their sites have been found in the park. The abandoned habitation sites range in size from one-room shelters to a 100-room pueblo near the Puerco River. Not all of them were occupied at the same time. Apparently, no one was living here permanently when the Spanish began their explorations of the Southwest in 1540, but there is documented evidence that roving bands of Zuni, Hopi, and Navajo people roamed this area after that date. Some of the Navajo even lived here at one time as shown by the ruins of a small group of hogans present in the northern part of the park.

We do not know whether any of the ancient people who once lived here recognized that some of the stone they fashioned into tools had originally been wood. However, Major John Wesley Powell, one of the early explorers of the Southwest, reported that the modern Paiute of southern Utah believed the petrified logs to be the arrow shafts of their thunder god, Shinuav. This may indicate that they had observed the similarity of the petrified logs to the trunks of living trees. On the other hand, the Navajo who lived in the vicinity of what is now the park believed that the logs were the bones of the monster Yietso, the Great Giant their ancestors slew when they first arrived in the Southwest.

**Opposite:** A natural bridge formed by a petrified log on top of Blue Mesa. **Top:** Large sandstone slabs provided abundant surface for the prehistoric inhabitants to leave many intricate and unique images carved into their exposed surfaces. **Above:** An assortment of arrowheads made of petrified wood. **Right:** Baje Whitethorne's painting depicts the encounter between Yietso and the first people.

Archaeologists have excavated some of the ancient habitation sites in the Petrified Forest. Just as fossils allow scientists to infer much about ancient plants and animals, building sites and associated artifacts tell us much about human life here in the past. Certain types of pottery, tools, and other artifacts help establish specific periods of occupation. Architectural styles, methods, and materials utilized in constructing houses and storage rooms also yield valuable information. Styles evolve or change as ideas spread from place to place. Meticulous study of these patterns of change and movement and of the structures and their contents tell us a great deal about the culture of the prehistoric inhabitants of the Petrified Forest.

As would be expected, early residents of what is now Petrified Forest National Park utilized many materials that they could obtain from nearby sources. For example, most dwellings, pottery, tools, and clothing used by the inhabitants of a Basketmaker II village, one of the oldest excavated sites in the park, were fashioned from such materials. Also, their foods were limited to plants they knew how to cultivate and to wild plants and animals that lived nearby. On the other hand, the turquoise, coral, and shell found at the sites must have been obtained by trade with other Native Americans, because they do not occur naturally in the park. And possibly, some of these early residents

may have even made pilgrimages to the Pacific Ocean and other sites where such exotic materials occurred. Perhaps the people who lived here traded petrified wood for those materials since stone tools made of similar petrified wood are found at many localities in the Southwest beyond the boundaries of the park.

Prehistoric inhabitants of the park were directly influenced by environmental changes. A dry year would mean poor crops and little food for the following winter. Their continued existence depended upon there being no drastic environmental changes of long duration. Even fairly minor changes in the amount and timing of rainfall could convert a fertile area into an uninhabitable one. Thus, during those years that the crops were good, they may have stored surpluses just as modern Puebloans do. Ancient storage facilities have been found at some of the habitation sites in the park and elsewhere in this region.

During the thirteenth century, a series of droughts occurred in southwestern North America that may have brought about the social collapse of the native cultures. Vegetation decreased and animal populations dwindled. Farming in many places became impossible, and the human population in those places could no longer endure. Either the people migrated or they perished. The great cliff dwellings, such as those in Mesa Verde National Park and hundreds of other villages in the Southwest, were abandoned at this time and never reoccupied.

In contrast, the extended period of drought seems to have only ended one way of life in the Petrified

**Top:** Ruins of a long-abandoned hogan built by Navajo people on the rim of the Painted Desert near the head of Lithodendron Wash. The walls were made from slabs of sandstone obtained from the Chinle Formation, and the roof and the upper parts of the walls, which consisted of logs and branches, have mostly disappeared. This hogan is one of a group of several old-style hogans built at this location most likely due to the nearby spring. **Bottom:** An ancient pot adorned with a handle used by long since gone residents of this arid land.

**Right:** Bowl and ladle, each with intricate decorations, are traces of a culture that once inhabited the area of the Petrified Forest National Park. **Below:** A careful examination of the large block of sandstone on the slope will reveal many petroglyphs, the largest of which is a large figure of a man. No doubt this block was still attached to the ledge of rock at the top of the slope when the petroglyphs were made.

Forest area while simultaneously stimulating the development of another. As the environment changed, the inhabitants of this region responded by developing new farming methods, new styles of construction, and new customs. The most obvious example of these changes is the Puerco Pueblo, constructed during the twelfth century and then enlarged during the great drought of the thirteenth century. Drought constituted a major environmental change that the native people could not control, but by adapting to this change, the residents of Puerco Pueblo were able to survive. Still later, however, additional environmental changes occurred that they could not cope with, and around 1380, the inhabitants were finally forced to abandon their homes and move elsewhere, possibly to the Hopi pueblos about 100 miles to the northwest or to the Zuni pueblos about the same distance to the east.

Wherever the displaced people went, it is unlikely that they ever returned to their old homes, because further and different changes began to occur in the middle 1500s. These changes were brought about by a series of invasions by more technologically advanced people. The invasions began with Spanish explorers en route to the Grand Canyon. Later, other explorers and missionaries from Spain and Mexico followed them. In time, these were succeeded by Euro–Americans who came from eastern North America and competed for land, water, and space. Occupation of their lands by people with such advanced technologies was still another change to which the native peoples in the area had to adjust.

What may be the oldest habitation site in the Petrified Forest to have been studied in detail is a small village on the top of a mesa in the southern portion of the park. This site, which was partially excavated during 1949, is thought to have been first occupied some time just prior to A.D. 500 during

what archaeologists usually call the Basketmaker II period. The village consisted of 25 round to oval pithouses scattered about the mesa top. The houses that were excavated had long, narrow east-facing entryways, and most were 9 to 12 feet in diameter. They had been dug 1 to 2 feet into the underlying rock material, and the underground portion had been lined with thin slabs of sandstone set on edge. It is probable that the upper part of the walls and the roof were made of brush and mud supported by juniper logs.

Many artifacts were found at this site including grinding stones, hammerstones, pipes, blades, scrapers, and numerous projectile points. About 60 percent of the stone artifacts were made of locally available materials such as sandstone, chert, and petrified wood. Abundant fragments of pottery also were found, and among the reconstructed vessels are bowls, jars of several sizes, ladles, and one vessel in the shape of a duck. Most of the pottery used by these people was gray–brown or tan to light red in color and was undecorated. The occurrence of pottery at such an old site is noteworthy.

**Left:** Displayed are ancient inscriptions carved into the sandstone's darker surface, desert varnish, an organic growth on the surface of the sandstone.
**Bottom and opposite:** *Tapamveni* is a Hopi word meaning "hammered mark" or "pounded sign," which is featured as the title of PFMA's award-winning rock art publication. These signposts abound in and around the Petrified Forest.

It is not known whether this village was a permanent place of residence or not. There is some evidence, but no proof, that it may have been occupied only during the summer while adjacent lands were farmed and that an unknown alternate site was occupied as a winter home.

Excavations at a somewhat later site demonstrate that cultural changes had taken place after the occupation of the Basketmaker II village described above. This site is on the floor of a broad valley and is usually classified as a Basketmaker III site. It may have been occupied from about A.D. 500 to possibly A.D. 800 and is different in several respects. It consists of at least 15 separate units scattered over an area approximately one-half mile square. The houses contain several innovations. For example, each unit is composed of one or more pithouses with several semi-subterranean storage structures, usually arranged in a crescent behind the pithouses. The pithouses were dug 3 to 4 feet into the ground. Posts supported the roof, which may have been constructed of brush and logs. Presumably, entry to these houses was gained via a hole in the roof. Of the several houses studied in detail, one had mud-plastered walls, while another had only sandstone slab walls more like the houses at the Basketmaker II site. Other innovations included small storage pits in the floor and a ventilator shaft at one side. Also, scattered about within the village are several apparently isolated semi-underground storage chambers.

Additional cultural changes were reflected in the styles of pottery, jewelry, and various implements found at this site. Stone tools had become more varied, and the style of projectile points had changed. Some of the pottery was a brown ware similar to that from Basketmaker II sites, but new ideas were making inroads on old customs, and some of the pottery was now decorated. In addition, a few pieces showed geometric designs or figures on the gray or white background. These people apparently practiced trade, as about half of the pottery found at the village was a plain brown ware similar to that made by the Mogollon (Muggy-YOWN) people to the south and east. It was probably obtained by trading, perhaps in exchange for articles made of petrified wood. Shell and bone articles like awls, needles, pendants, beads, and bracelets were also found at the Basketmaker III site. The shells were of marine origin and probably came from the Gulf of California and the Pacific Ocean—another indication that the inhabitants of the village had engaged in trading.

Eight human burials were unearthed during excavations at the village. All were very poorly preserved and consisted of only a few bones. The dead had been placed in their grave lying on their back with knees flexed and their head oriented to the west or southwest. Pottery, fur blankets, awls, beads, pendants, and bracelets were among the items found with the burials. These grave goods probably indicate that the people of this village had ceremonial burial practices.

Adjacent to the village are low stone structures that might have been part of windbreaks in patches of farmed land. Modern Hopi farmers use similar windbreaks to reduce movement of windblown sand onto their fields. Such windbreaks probably also reduce moisture loss by slowing air movement across the fields. If these structures were, in fact, related to farming, it indicates that summer rainfall was adequate enough to support crops.

There is no evidence of any other source of water for crops such as irrigation canals or wells. Some of the farmlands are located on hillsides, where water retention would not have been great. Farmlands in these locations would have taken advantage of sheet wash that occurred after rainstorms.

The apparent close-knit organization of the village, the large food-storage structures, and other factors indicate that it was occupied all year. This contrasts with the situation at the Basketmaker II period village site, which probably was occupied only part of the year.

**Above:** Pendants made of shell were probably brought from the Pacific Ocean for trading purposes. **Below:** Some of the men of the CCC who helped build the Painted Desert Inn and reconstruct Agate House, the small pueblo in the southern part of the park shown on the opposite page.

## Roosevelt's Tree Army    *by Rita Garcia, Interpretive Ranger, Petrified Forest National Park*

THE STOCK MARKET CRASHED. The country's economy is in a shambles. Unemployment is at 80% in some Eastern urban areas. Add to these factors a terrible drought, extreme soil erosion from the Dustbowl throughout the middle United States, and large expanses of forestlands wiped out by timber clear-cutting. This was the state of the Union during the Great Depression of the 1930s.

Franklin Delano Roosevelt won the presidency in 1932 by promising to fix the nation's woes through the Emergency Conservation Work Act. This program, which led to the Civilian Conservation Corps (CCC), proposed to recruit unemployed young men, enroll them in a peacetime army, and send them out to do battle against destruction and erosion of the country's natural resources. It would become one of the most successful relief programs in the history of the United States.

Petrified Forest National Park provides numerous examples of the remarkable work done by the men of the Civilian Conservation Corps, which was also called the Tree Army. Most of the park road, many of the bridges, and some of the trails still used today can be credited to the CCC. The park's water distribution system, the Rainbow Forest Museum and ranger residences, and the 1930's renovation of the beautiful Painted Desert Inn Museum all get credited to the hard work of the enrollees. Even some of the striking exhibits in the Rainbow Forest Museum and the fairground's grandstand in the nearby town of Holbrook were built courtesy of the CCC.

To get an idea of just how much the enrollees accomplished, one need only look at the Painted Desert Inn. Money and machinery were scarce during the Depression, so human hands did almost all of the work: digging trenches, quarrying rock, chiseling flagstone, and building masonry walls that averaged 27 inches in thickness. The men of the CCC shaped tree trunks into window frames, ceiling beams, restaurant tables, chairs, a complete soda fountain bar with stools, decorative corbels, grills, and doors. Enrollees cut and shaped tin into light fixtures and then hand-punched festive patterns into the tin. Hand-painted glass panels depicting symbols based on ancient American Indian pottery designs became a lovely skylight in the main trading post room. The entire building currently exists as a work of art and stands today as a memorial to the impressive work completed by the CCC. Further examples of their skill and hard work are found in the beautiful stonewalls of many of the older buildings in the park, especially in the Rainbow Forest area. The stone blocks in the walls were quarried and shaped by the CCC men, who then carefully laid them in hand-mixed mortar.

Although the Civilian Conservation Corps was disbanded in 1942, visitors to Petrified Forest National Park and other parks across the country still benefit from their labors. As you travel through this park or others, take some time to look at the trails, bridges, and buildings around you. They aren't just structures—they are an important part of our nation's history.

## Agate House

Agate House is an eight-room pueblo situated on top of a low knoll in Rainbow Forest. Like several other pueblos in the park, it had been built almost entirely of blocks of petrified wood laid in adobe mortar. Pottery and artifacts found during excavation indicate that Agate House was constructed and used during the Pueblo III period. Because of its small size and the limited number of artifacts and pottery found at the site, Agate House might have been occupied for only a short time. The form and type of construction of Agate House are signs of the cultural changes that took place after the Basketmaker III village mentioned previously had been occupied. The inhabitants now lived in dwellings that were attached to each other, not scattered about or partially dug out of the ground.

## Puerco Pueblo

A series of droughts beginning in A.D. 1215 and continuing until 1299 caused major changes in the native cultures of the Southwest. What had been a dispersed population living in small villages and isolated dwellings could no longer persist. As weather patterns altered, adaptation to the changing environment became necessary for survival. The old ways of life were no longer adequate, so new customs and styles evolved.

Although summer rains were no longer sufficient to support farming everywhere, some areas in the region remained habitable. Along major drainages like the Puerco River, there was enough moisture available between rains, which permitted farming to continue. Consequently, people gradually congregated at a few sites near the more dependable water supplies and abandoned the many scattered small villages and summer farming sites. In other places, permanent villages developed and expanded.

The ruins of one such permanent village are near the intersection of the main park road and the Puerco River. They are the remains of a 100-room pueblo now called the Puerco Ruin. Apparently, the site was first occupied around A. D. 1250 during late Pueblo III times. The settlement then experienced rapid growth during early Pueblo IV times, and at its largest size around A. D. 1300, the pueblo had an estimated population of about 200. Then the population of the pueblo began to decline, and it was eventually abandoned permanently around A. D. 1380. Puerco Pueblo was a farming community with cultural ties to other villages in the region. The inhabitants farmed the floodplain and terraces along the Puerco River, where their crops of corn, beans, and squash could find adequate moisture even though the river itself was often dry. Their diet was supplemented with wild plants and game.

Puerco Pueblo was built primarily of stone blocks, with rooms arranged around a large plaza containing several underground ceremonial chambers, or kivas (KEE-vahs). The ruin has not been completely excavated, but it appears that there were at least two to three rows of rooms around the plaza on the west and south sides, but only a single row of rooms along the north and east walls.

A portion of Puerco Indian Ruin showing typical rooms built with slabs of sandstone laid in adobe mortar. The beautiful valley of the Rio Puerco is in the middle ground to the left.

Part of the pueblo may have been two stories high. Rooms on the outside were primarily storage rooms, while those on the inside rows were mostly living quarters. There were no doors or windows in the exterior walls of the pueblo, but there may have been gateways in the north and west walls. Entry to most of the rooms was through holes or hatchways in the log, brush, and mud roof. Possible doorways have been discovered in the walls of some of the rooms. Within each house unit in the pueblo, the occupants could move from room to room by way of very small doorways in the interior walls.

Puerco Pueblo was occupied during the severe recurring droughts of the 1200s. The altered way of life, which must have been accompanied by many cultural changes, was an adaptation that permitted the inhabitants to remain here 100 to 200 years longer than would have otherwise been possible.

Following the dry spells of the 1200s, weather patterns changed. Rainfall increased greatly in the late 1300s, but instead of reverting to the pre-1200 weather pattern, much of the annual precipitation occurred in the winter months and was no longer distributed throughout spring and summer as it had been. What rain now fell in summer was probably concentrated in short, violent thunderstorms.

With increasing winter precipitation and heavy summer storms, the Puerco River began to actively erode the terraces along its banks, a process that gradually eliminated the adjacent farmlands. Adjustment to these environmental changes now became necessary. The villagers depended upon the crops that were planted upon the floodplain terraces, because the summer weather patterns prevented farming elsewhere. As a consequence of erosion of the terraces, food production decreased.

Unable to adapt to the change in environment that eliminated their crops, the inhabitants of Puerco Pueblo had the option of remaining and dying or moving in search of a more suitable area. It appears that around A. D. 1380 the inhabitants systematically abandoned the Pueblo. There is no evidence that the residents were driven away by conflict, no evidence of battles, and no evidence of an epidemic. Recent excavations indicate that the last seven or eight families to leave the pueblo purposely burned their living quarters and remaining foodstores. According to Hopi tradition, Puerco villagers moved northwest to the Hopi pueblos, which have survived to the present.

**Above:** The feet of the mountain lion in this petroglyph seem a bit exaggerated; otherwise, the figure is quite lifelike.

# A Rock Art Legacy

Much evidence of Native American activities is found in the Petrified Forest. For example, at certain outcrops of coarse sandstone that was pulverized to mix with pottery clay, hammerstones still lie just as they were left several hundred years ago. Broken bits of pottery litter the ground in the vicinity of ruins. At several places there are chipping stations where Native Americans manufactured tools from petrified wood and rock.

Throughout the park there are thousands of petroglyphs, or rock drawings. They were made by chiseling through the dark brown patina, known as desert varnish that occurs on the surfaces of sandstone. The patina is formed by weathering and affects only a thin outer layer of the rock. Beneath this layer the rock is lighter in color, so designs usually show clearly where the patina has been removed. Much of the inspiration for the petroglyphs has come from nature, although they often include simple to complex geometric patterns. Human and animal figures from tiny to almost life-size and many unidentified designs also occur. Some may have ceremonial or historical meaning, and others may simply be doodling or of sexual significance.

Several of the petroglyphs seem to be solar calendars. These figures are usually spiral or circular in design. At the solstices and/or equinoxes, a bar of sunlight moves across the pattern until it touches the center. Some exhibit other precise interactions with sunlight. Apparently, the Native Americans who made the designs could determine the precise time of the winter and summer solstices and the spring and autumn equinoxes, important information for the farmers that inhabited the area.

There are two places in the park where petroglyphs may be easily viewed. One of these is at Newspaper Rock, where rock surfaces are covered with thousands of petroglyphs. Another site is along the cliff on the east side of Puerco Ruin. They are also present in the park at other locations along many of the escarpments where beds of hard sandstone in the Chinle Formation are exposed.

It is not possible to determine the age of individual petroglyphs. The rate at which desert varnish develops depends upon so many variables that it is of no use in measuring time. However, petroglyphs vary in clarity, so it is obvious that they also vary somewhat in age. In some cases, newer petroglyphs partially obscure older ones. Possibly a design or a figure made at one time may be adjacent to one made several years later, yet it appears to be of similar age. Different individuals representing different cultures could have made two petroglyphs of the same age. And in other situations one artist may well have decided to "improve" the work of another.

In places, groups of petroglyphs occur on smooth rock faces 12 to 15 feet above ground level. With no handholds or ledges, how could the artist have executed his work at that height? He probably did it by standing on the ground, and erosion has since washed away the surface on which he stood, gradually lowering it to its present level. In some cases, a slab of rock that has since fallen to the ground might have provided a foothold for that artist hundreds of years ago.

**Right:** A nicely formed but somewhat stylized petroglyph of a human being. **Below:** This slab of sandstone is densely covered with a variety of petroglyphs, some of which are clearly identifiable.

# Petrified Forest Today

**Opposite:** Onyx Bridge in the Black Forest. This natural bridge collapsed several years after this picture was taken. The wood in this log is noticeably darker than the logs in the southern part of the park.

**Top:** A coyote on the prowl. Coyotes are important members of the food chain in the park, because they help control rodent populations.

**Bottom:** Bikers Peter Fonda and Dennis Hopper cruise through the badlands of the Petrified Forest in the 1969 classic hit *Easy Rider*.

VISITORS TO NORTHEASTERN ARIZONA are often surprised by the vegetation of the area, because it consists predominantly of grass and brush. "But where are the cactus?" is a common question from newcomers to northeastern Arizona. Cactus do grow here, but it is limited to small, often inconspicuous species. The saguaro and organ pipe cacti and the Joshua tree and other distinctive succulents are limited to the deserts south and west of the Petrified Forest.

Residents of Arizona's northeastern plateau often speak of their surroundings as desert, but technically, the vegetation type here is short grass plains or desert shrub. The term desert grassland is also often used. Whatever one calls it, the area contains a complex and fascinating combination of plants and animals. To many people, terms such as "barren," "desolate,"

and even "dull" seem an appropriate description. But to those who know it, or to those who will look at it with an inquiring eye, this land is filled with life, color, and form.

Climate sets the theme here, as it does everywhere. Wind and water carve the landscape. They help create soils and remove them, thus assisting in controlling the plants that grow here. Moisture, sunlight, temperature, and wind all impose further limitations on the vegetation. In turn, vegetation and climate greatly influence the selection of animals that can survive here. Some animals control the survival of other animals and even of certain plants. This is not a straight chain of single links but a mesh, a web of life, supported by air, light, land, and water and influenced by every strand of the web.

Each part of the web helps hold the others above the abyss of extinction. Small parts of the web, even individual strands, may fall or disappear without danger to the whole. But if enough strands are broken, the remaining parts will be too weak to support the rest, and the web will collapse.

In the Petrified Forest, the climate is one of extremes and occasional violence. Annual precipitation averages about 9 inches—most major U.S. cities receive 25 to 50 inches—and half of it comes in short, violent thunderstorms in July, August, and September. The other half of the year's precipitation is received in rain and snow showers scattered throughout the rest of the year. May, June, and sometimes early July are usually very dry.

Brief snowstorms are not uncommon in the winter, but the snow is rarely deep and seldom remains very long. Sub-zero temperatures often occur during winter nights, and even in bright sunshine, subfreezing temperatures can persist all day. Moderate afternoon temperatures are not unusual in midwinter.

Summer daytime temperatures average in the low 90s, rising gradually to 100 degrees Fahrenheit or more for a few days in July. As in most high desert and grassland areas, nighttime temperatures are much cooler.

**Above:** After a rare snowstorm, the Painted Desert takes on a new and special appearance. **Below:** An alert collared lizard sunning itself. These are some of the largest lizards found in the park. **Right:** A summer thunder shower in the colorful Painted Desert. In the right background, Chinde Mesa rises up above the scene.

High winds may occur at any time; they typically create dust and sandstorms along dry stream beds and over denuded land. Where grass and brush are not excluded by natural constraints or have not been destroyed by man's influence, blowing sand and dust are seldom a problem.

Climate, with other influences, selects the vegetation and wildlife that live on the land. Plants must evolve very efficient methods of collection and storage of water to survive in an area of such limited rainfall. In addition, they must compete with their neighbor for what moisture becomes available. Perennial plants collect some water during even the driest part of the year, while annuals must pass the dry seasons in a dormant form, such as a seed.

Plants have also evolved other survival strategies, including the development on their leaves of a waxy waterproofing called cuticle, which reduces moisture loss. A few plants even share the leafless habit of cacti. Mormon tea, a common shrub in this area, consists of jointed green twigs with tiny scale-like leaves. Annual plants that pass the winter as seeds and many grasses that over-winter in a dormant condition avoid the water shortage in dry summers simply by not growing. The seeds and dormant plants remain in that state until the next year brings rain.

Cacti and some other plants may utilize a widespread shallow root system to absorb great quantities of water near the surface during rains, and then store it in their fleshy stems. Other plants may store water in their thick, fleshy roots. Some animals that would eat cacti for food or for the stored moisture are deterred by the sharp spines.

Yucca (YUK-ah) plants, even more than cacti, are typical of the southwestern flora. Two species of yucca are present in the Petrified Forest, and their relatives are found throughout the arid Southwest. Yuccas were, and still are, much used by Native Americans for the plants provide several products they use. The long, thin, needle-sharp leaves provide fibers for weaving; the root is used for preparing soap; and the fat seed pods are consumed as food.

Grasses in this area do not usually carpet the ground like a lawn or an eastern grassland. What may first appear to be an unbroken mat of vegetation is, in fact, a large number of individual plants separated from their neighbors by bare ground. This regular spacing of plants may result from competition for moisture or from a defensive adaptation that prohibits the growth of other plants. If water competition causes the spacing, it simply means that under the conditions at that place there is only enough water to support the plants that are already there. New plants cannot establish themselves in the open ground because the roots of older plants absorb all the water. Thus, new plants may start to grow, but they quickly die from lack of moisture. Should an older plant die or be removed, a replacement will shortly spring up in the same place.

**Left:** With their lustrous black plumage and loud harsh calls ravens are easily recognized. They are commonly found searching for food near parking and picnic areas in the park. **Below:** Long Logs section of Rainbow Forest on a summer day. Shadows of the clouds give this scene a distinctive look.

**Right:** An alert Prairie dog is constantly on guard against predators such as coyotes, large snakes, and birds like Golden Eagles.

Some plants have evolved a more sophisticated adaptation that carries them a step farther. Chemical compounds produced by their roots or released by their decaying leaves prevent other plants from growing nearby. Still other plants are prevented from growing too close by an inhibitor that slows root growth or by a toxin that kills the competitor outright.

Plants in any area must adapt to survive changing conditions, and they must do so where they grow. Animals must also adapt to their environment, but they can move away from inhospitable changes. They rarely move far, however, and either adapt to their surroundings or die. Normally, the environment changes slowly, and all inhabitants must either evolve over many generations or they perish. If environmental changes should occur rapidly, however, the survival of any species becomes highly unlikely.

Migration over long distances is one adaptation to the changing seasons. Most summer-resident birds in the Petrified Forest are dependent upon a diet of live insects. Such birds depart for southern regions about the time the insect supply declines in autumn. Other birds adapt to the changing seasons by shifting from a summer diet of insects to one of seeds in the winter.

Unable to migrate, small mammals in the park have evolved other survival techniques such as food storage and hibernation. Many rodents store fruit, seeds, or dried vegetation in underground chambers. Then, they sleep through most of the winter without going into true hibernation, awakening occasionally to feed. Mammals that do hibernate live on food stored as fat within their bodies, and their bodily processes— heartbeat, circulation, breathing—slow to a very low level. The animals seem to be in suspended animation rather than asleep.

Reptiles and amphibians in the Petrified Forest share the hibernation habit. The common gopher snake, which is large and handsomely patterned, the brightly-colored milk snake, and the rarely seen western rattlesnake disappear in fall and are not seen again until spring, when they emerge from their underground dens.

The harmless gopher snake is found throughout the park and may hiss loudly and vibrate its tail like a rattlesnake if it is startled. This snake eats a variety of prey, including insects, birds, bird eggs, lizards, mice, and carrion. As the name indicates, the western rattlesnake (also called the Hopi rattlesnake) has a rattle at the end of its tail, which it shakes vigorously when threatened. It normally frequents the grasslands and piñon-juniper habitats in the park and has a diet similar to that of the gopher snake. Unlike some other snakes, the western rattler bears live young in late summer. Rattlesnakes pose little threat to park visitors, because they are shy and usually will not strike unless cornered or provoked.

Many species of lizards are present throughout the park, and summer visitors are likely to see them any place they stop. However, they disappear from the scene each winter, as do the toads and salamanders.

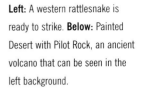

**Left:** A western rattlesnake is ready to strike. **Below:** Painted Desert with Pilot Rock, an ancient volcano that can be seen in the left background.

One of the most frequently observed lizards is the eastern fence lizard, which is found in every habitat in the park. It has chevrons or crescents down its back and has light brown or tan stripes on the sides. Another common lizard in the park is the brilliantly colored collard lizard that has green highlights on its back and a double black neck collar. It has sharp teeth and is noted for its predatory habits, eating other lizards, insects, and small mammals, as well as berries and flowers. Although this lizard usually lives in rocky areas where it often perches on boulders or petrified logs, it has also been observed in grasslands and sand dunes in the park. When startled, this lizard may run away on its hind feet with its front legs and tail raised off the ground like a miniature bipedal dinosaur.

Although seven species of amphibians are present in the park, they are rarely seen by casual visitors because they are normally active only during the wet periods of the year in the vicinity of standing water. Typically, many utilize temporary pools that fill with water when it rains and develop very quickly. For example, Couch's spadefoot toad can go from egg to adult in as little as 9 days. Other amphibians such as the true toads and the salamander take longer to develop and must use more permanent bodies of water in the Puerco River, stock tanks, etc., as breeding places. During the non-breeding season, the amphibians survive by hiding underground in burrows they have dug or in burrows made by other animals. They may be inactive for 11 months of the year.

Predators, both birds and mammals, undergo little change in what they eat, but they may experience difficulty in finding enough food during the winter. Bobcats, coyotes, and foxes range farther and spend more hours seeking jackrabbits, cottontails, birds, and other prey in winter.

Since there are no lakes or permanent streams in the park, water supply is as much a problem for animals as it is for plants. The adaptations of wildlife to the arid environment are many and varied. Some of the large mammals such as the pronghorn antelope and wide-ranging birds like the golden eagle and the raven may periodically visit water holes outside the park. The kangaroo rat has evolved a very sophisticated adaptation to aridity—it manufactures water. This unique ability to chemically manufacture water while living on a diet of dry food, together with an extremely efficient urinary system that conserves water in the body, makes the kangaroo rat quite independent of liquid water supplies. During the summer rainy season, there is usually an ample water supply within the boundaries of the Petrified Forest, but during most of the year and in the occasional summer drought, water supplies may be critical.

Dew, frost, and snow provide an irregular supply of moisture that may be adequate for some animals.

The varied plants and animals of the Petrified Forest of 225 million years ago were also supported by the web of life. But as time passed, conditions changed. For the dinosaurs these changes were for the better, and they went on to dominate the land for nearly 150 million years. However, other inhabitants of that ancient world, such as the phytosaurs, were unable to keep pace with the changes and soon became extinct. As time passed, plants also changed in response to environmental alterations, at least in part, with some groups either adapting or becoming extinct. These changes eventually culminated 100 million years later in the appearance of flowering plants.

The Native Americans who had lived in the Petrified Forest for hundreds of years were forced to leave the area when changes in the climate occurred. Today, armed with our increasingly sophisticated technology, the stresses we place on the web of life are more severe. But this same technology also allows us to study and learn about this web. We are caught up in a race of global proportions. Which will win—our ability to tear the web apart, or our ability to study, understand, and preserve it?

Today, the wisdom of placing the petrified forests under governmental protection is undisputed. Commercial interests and souvenir collecting have greatly depleted the deposits of petrified wood in areas surrounding the park. The foresight of the conservationists of the late 1800s and early 1900s has preserved this resource for the pleasure and enjoyment of today's visitor and the use of scientists. Protection of the other fossils has given us a chance to look at the plants and animals of more than 225 million years ago, while the preservation of archaeological resources permits us to study how people managed to survive in this apparently inhospitable desert environment.

Others may obtain enough moisture from edible plants. In dry periods, some creatures may force their way past cactus spines to eat the spongy, wet tissues of the plant. Water is usually close to the surface in dry stream beds, and bobcats and coyotes have been known to dig holes there to find water.

The desert grassland web of life, supported like other webs by soil, water, air, and light, is a resilient network that has evolved over eons of time. Early Native American peoples in the area lived a life integrated in the web. More recently, we have imposed new tensions and pressures on the web. The introduction of new wildlife such as cattle, sheep, goats, horses, and burros has wrenched entire sections of the web into a new shape that probably cannot long endure. The overutilization of some food plants by stock has opened the way for the proliferation of other plants, some of which may become pests. Vegetation changes force immediate and large-scale changes in wildlife—some species disappear and others increase explosively. Each change triggers others, and as ecology runs wild, the web of life trembles.

In some places, the overuse of land has removed the protective vegetation, thus greatly increasing soil erosion. Where much moisture was once absorbed, water and tons of soil now run off rapidly. Downstream the silt mixes with sewage and industrial pollutants, and the water becomes unfit for human use. Most windblown soil settles back to earth, but a small amount is carried aloft where it absorbs a tiny but significant amount of sunlight. There it also mixes with pollutants that combine chemically with the oxygen that is so critical to all animal life.

**Above:** Short sections of logs that have recently been exposed when the surrounding rocks were washed away. **Right:** A wary cottontail rabbit. These mammals have a white tail and feed on grass and other green plants late in the day and early in the morning.

The National Park Service continues the struggle to preserve the petrified wood and other resources for the future. No longer is petrified wood hauled out of the park by the boxcar load, nor do thoughtless and selfish persons blast open logs in hopes of finding valuable crystals. Today, no one proposes that the wood be converted to abrasives. Nevertheless, an estimated 25,000 pounds of wood are removed from the park each year. Bit by bit, pieces of wood are removed by basically honest people who would not think of stealing a candy bar from the grocery store or a newspaper from an unattended stand. Petty shoplifting is bad enough; it is the theft of replaceable manufactured items from an individual. Petrified wood thieves, on the other hand, are stealing an irreplaceable monument to 225 million years of development, and they are stealing it from all of us.

## Exploration and Development

The presence of petrified wood in the Chinle Formation in what is now Petrified Forest National Park did not become generally known until about the middle of the nineteenth century. Previously, several Spanish explorers had crossed the Painted Desert, but they apparently did not see or did not recognize the petrified wood in that area. Captain Lorenzo Sitgreaves of the U.S. Army appears to have been the first person to publish a description of petrified wood in the vicinity of the park. He discovered it on September 28, 1851, in an area several miles south of what is now the park while he was leading an army exploring expedition through parts of western New Mexico and eastern Arizona.

In 1853, members of the U. S. Army exploring expedition led by Lieutenant Amiel W. Whipple discovered the large deposit of wood in the northern part of Petrified Forest National Park that is now known as the Black Forest. An early description of that forest was published in 1855 in a report on the expedition, together with the first picture of a scene in today's park. Whipple was so impressed by the petrified wood that he named the arroyo in the vicinity of the deposit Lithodendron (Stonetree) Wash.

A few years later in 1858, a U. S. Army exploring expedition led by Lieutenant J. C. Ives crossed broad exposures of the brightly colored Chinle Formation some 50 miles north of Lithodendron Wash. The members were so impressed by the striking colors of the area that they named it the Painted Desert.

Within a few years, other petrified forests in the vicinity of Lithodendron Wash were discovered, and interest in them developed very quickly as news of them spread by word of mouth, through books, and through newspapers. In the autumn of 1878, U.S. Army General William T. Sherman, while on a tour of military posts in the West, suggested to the commanding officer of Fort Wingate in western New Mexico that two of the famous petrified logs be collected for the Smithsonian Institution in Washington. Accordingly, the next spring a small detail under the command of Lieutenant John E. C. Hegewald was sent from Fort Wingate, New Mexico, to collect them.

After the trip, the detail arrived at Bear Spring near Lithodendron Wash where they set up camp. Also camped nearby were a number of Navajo Indians, who, according to Hegewald, ". . . thought it strange the 'Great Father in Washington' should want some of the bones of the 'Great Giant' their forefathers had killed when taking possession of the country. . ."

**Top Left:** A striking example of the beautiful plant commonly known as Indian Paintbrush. Reportedly, some Native Americans use this plant in ceremonies and for medicine.
**Bottom Left:** A solitary pronghorn. In the park, they are typically found south of Interstate 40 foraging for food such as grass and sagebrush.

# The Painted Desert Inn

The Painted Desert Inn is one of the most attractive historic buildings in the park. Herbert D. Lore, a local businessman, built the original structure using blocks of petrified wood and local stone. Originally called the "Stone-Tree House," Lore's facility opened in 1924 and offered everything a weary, dusty traveler needed, including a lunchroom, curio shop, and bar. Even a few small rooms were available for overnight stay. Lore also offered short motorcar tours into the Painted Desert and over to the Black Forest. Interestingly, the remains of some of the dirt trails he developed are still visible in the Painted Desert below the rim.

Stone Tree House attracted many travelers due to the spectacular views it provided of the Painted Desert. Also, it was more appealing than the majority of the unsightly, rundown cafes, curio shops, and service stations built along Route 66. For over a decade tourists and other travelers visited the Painted Desert Inn, purchasing food and curios and exploring the Painted Desert. In the early 1930s, a series of events began which eventually resulted in a change of ownership, appearance, and even use of the building. First, in 1932, 53,300 acres of the Painted Desert north of Lore's facility were added to the Petrified Forest National Monument, doubling it in size. Then, in 1935, after several years of negotiation Lore sold the building and his land on the edge of the Painted Desert to the federal government.

The National Park Service chose to modernize, enlarge, and generally make the facility more attractive prior to reopening for business, so remodeling began in May of 1937 by members of the Civilian Conservation Corps. They followed plans drawn by National Park Service architect Lyle Bennett, who wanted to give the building a Spanish Pueblo Revival appearance. In keeping with this design, the gabled roof of the original structure was removed and replaced with a flat roof. Ponderosa pine logs obtained from Flagstaff, Arizona, were used for roofing beams and aspen poles from the White Mountains were used as crossbeams. The walls were covered inside and out with a thick layer of brownish cement stucco that resembled the mud used on the walls of nearby Pueblos. Handmade Mexican-style tin light fixtures were installed throughout the building. Tables and chairs were constructed and carved with Native American designs. Glass skylight panels were installed in the ceiling over the main room on the top floor and handpainted with designs inspired by ancient pottery. The concrete floors in some rooms were engraved with geometric figures modeled after Navajo blanket designs.

Finally, the remodeling was complete and the Painted Desert Inn, as the building was now called, reopened for business on July 4, 1940, with part of it being used as the visitor center for the north end of the park. Once again, the facility provided weary travelers on Route 66 with food, drink, and lodging, as well as curios and information.

Due to the lack of civilian travel during World War II, the Inn closed again in October 1942. In April 1947, the business portion of the Inn was reopened and managed by the Fred Harvey Company. Shortly thereafter, the company's architect and designer, Mary Colter, changed the color scheme and had large plate glass windows installed in some of the walls to take advantage of the striking views of the Painted Desert. At her suggestion the famous Hopi artist Fred Kabotie was hired to paint murals on the walls in the dining room and lunchroom.

In 1963, after many years of successful operation, the Painted Desert Inn closed again when the Fred Harvey Company moved its operation to the new park headquarters that had just been completed about two miles south of the Painted Desert Inn. Due to the clay under the foundation, the Inn quickly began to deteriorate as the walls continued to crack and shift and leaks developed in the roof. Soon there were calls for the building to be demolished. Fortunately, in 1975, the Inn was placed on the National Register of Historic Places, and in 1976, it was repaired enough to use as the Petrified Forest National Park Bicentennial Travel Center. In 1987, it was designated a National Historic Landmark and its future was assured. Since that time much additional stabilization work has taken place and the roof has been repaired. In 1990, the doors to the Inn were opened once again and offered visitors a museum, information center, and sales area. Ongoing efforts continue to rehabilitate the building, its roof, and interior, including an extensive rehabilitation of the building in 2004-2005.

**Above:** A selection of the recently-restored, hand-painted skylight panels found in the Painted Desert Inn. **Background:** Painted Desert Inn at sunset with the shadow-filled Painted Desert in the distance.

A Large Petrified Tree. Adamana, Arizona.

## Adamana and the Beginnings of Tourism in the Petrified Forest

Modern tourism really began in the Petrified Forest when Adamana Station was built a short distance west of the future park by the Atchison, Topeka, and Santa Fe Railroad in 1890. Named for Adam and Anna Hanna who owned an adjacent ranch, the station was built to service the railroad and facilitate tours of the Petrified Forest, then called Chalcedony Park, for interested train passengers. Prior to that time visitors to the park were mostly locals who participated in informal excursions led by local guides, and it was only after Adamana was founded that guided trips became organized and advertised.

A major promoter of this enterprise was the Santa Fe Railroad, which extensively advertised tours and gladly arranged stopovers for their passengers. As a result, visitation increased rapidly. At first, tourists were met at the train and taken to Hanna's nearby ranch house, where they could stay overnight and take guided trips into Chalcedony Park. Later, as visitation increased, Hanna built a hotel near the railroad tracks and hired a local rancher, Al Stevenson, to manage the new facility, which they named the Forest Hotel. It could lodge up to twenty guests and had a dining room that sat thirty. Account books for the hotel show that a night's lodging cost $2.00 and $2.50 for both room and board. As time passed, a small settlement developed near the hotel for employees and their families and a school was established for their children.

For several years, both Hanna and Stevenson continued to lead increasingly popular tours into Chalcedony Park. According to the guest register at the Forest Hotel, nearly a thousand tourists visited it in 1902. By 1907, the numbers had more than doubled, and by 1915, about 5700 tourists visited the park.

During this period, one of the most notable guests was the famous naturalist John Muir, who, with his two daughters, lived there for nearly a year from late 1905 until August 1906. While in the area Muir explored the petrified forests and collected fossilized bones and teeth of Late Triassic amphibians. These were given to the University of California at Berkeley, where they became the nucleus of the vertebrate collections in the Museum of Paleontology. As a consequence of Muir's findings, vertebrate paleontologists became aware of the fossil treasures present in the rocks surrounding Adamana, and they too began to take advantage of the facilities when working in the area. Eventually, their work helped to increase interest in the park and entice more tourists to visit the reserve.

After Petrified Forest National Monument was established in 1906, Al Stevenson was appointed its custodian because of his vast knowledge of the reserve. He received $1.00 per month for his trouble. Since Stevenson still managed the hotel, Adamana became the unofficial headquarters of the new monument. In 1907, Hanna sold the Forest Hotel to Stevenson who tried to make trips in the monument more comfortable for tourists by improving the unpaved roads and building bridges. Unfortunately, improvements such as these were made at his own expense since the federal government refused to support such work. Stevenson sold the hotel in 1913 and was succeeded by a series of men who also managed the hotel and the monument.

For a time, the future seemed bright for both the monument and hotel as visitation continued to increase, but then, as highways in the area were developed and improved, more and more visitors began arriving by automobile and eventually they outnumbered those traveling by train. As a result, fewer tourists utilized the hotel in Adamana each year. Until the early 1920s, Adamana had been the principal gateway to the reserve and one of only a few tourism operations near the monument. However, this changed when other northern Arizona residents began to develop tourist facilities along the newly designated and improved U.S. Highway 66 and competition for the tourist dollar became fierce. A major competitor was the Painted Desert Inn (then called Stone Tree House) built near the highway on the edge of the Painted Desert to the north. The final decline of Adamana was brought about in 1930 by the building of a bridge across the Puerco River about 2 miles to the east. Thereafter, tourists could drive directly from U.S. Highway 66 into the monument on an improved all-weather road. As a result, Adamana was no longer the entryway to Petrified Forest National Monument, nor were its tourist facilities needed. Adamana remains today as one of Arizona's ghost towns— just a name on a map with its tourist population replaced by tumbleweeds.

3126. Stage Leaving for Forests, Adamana, Arizona.

Two segments of a partly buried log that fit the requirements outlined by General Sherman were located about one and a quarter miles below Bear Spring. Both segments were loaded onto wagons and hauled to Fort Wingate. At least one of the specimens was shipped to the Smithsonian and was subsequently put on display in the U.S. National Museum of Natural History together with another log from the Chinle Formation near Fort Wingate.

In 1883, the Atlantic and Pacific Railroad was completed through northern Arizona, following the course of the Puerco River through what was to become Petrified Forest National Park. With completion of the railway, travel through northern Arizona increased rapidly, and the population of the region began to grow as new settlers arrived and established homesteads nearby. At the same time, the petrified forests became the object of rapidly increasing visitation by local residents and tourists alike.

About one mile west of Puerco Ruin, the town of Adamana was founded in 1890. It provided a place where transcontinental trains could stop to take on water and coal and where passengers could dine. Soon Adamana also became the headquarters for tours of the petrified forests, and a hotel was built there to accommodate tourists' needs. One of the more famous tourists of the time was the naturalist John Muir. He stayed in Adamana for several months in 1905-1906 with his daughters. While there, he explored the petrified forests and collected a small number of bones, which he donated to the University of California Museum of Paleontology. At this time, the Santa Fe Railway, successor to the Atlantic and Pacific, encouraged passengers to visit the petrified forests and even published brochures advertising them.

As visitation increased, larger and larger amounts of petrified wood were carried off. It was reported that railway boxcar-loads of petrified wood were shipped to the eastern United States, so that it could be made into tabletops, mantel pieces, and ornaments of various types. Large logs were often dynamited by people searching for amethysts and other crystals. At Adamana, a mill was built for the purpose of crushing petrified wood into abrasives. Although the mill never went into operation because of the development of cheaper abrasives, this incident convinced some Arizona residents that the petrified forests would soon disappear unless they were protected by the federal government. Therefore, in 1895, the Arizona territorial legislature petitioned the U.S. Congress to have the area containing the petrified forests set aside as a national park.

Lester F. Ward, a paleobotanist with the U.S. Geological Survey, examined the area in 1899 and recommended that it be withdrawn from entry by homesteaders and established as a national park. On December 8, 1906, President Theodore Roosevelt used the newly passed Antiquities Act to set aside the nation's second national monument–Petrified Forest. Boundary changes have been made several times since 1906, including the addition of the Painted Desert Section in 1932. Legislation was passed in 1958 to establish the area as a national park to protect not only the petrified wood but also the other fossils, the archaeological sites, the scenery, and the desert plants and animals.

In 1962, the area was designated as Petrified Forest National Park, and in 2004, the boundaries were extended to include large areas on both the eastern and western sides. As a result, the size of the park was more than doubled and vast quantities of virtually unexplored natural resources have been preserved for scientific study and enjoyment by the American people.

## Suggested Reading

### SETTING THE GEOLOGIC SCENE

Baars, Donald L., *The Colorado Plateau: A geologic history*. Albuquerque, New Mexico: University of New Mexico Press, 1998.

Bezy, John V. and Trevena, A. S., *Guide to geologic features at Petrified Forest National Park*. Tucson, Arizona: Arizona Geological Survey, 2000.

Breed, William J. and Breed, Carol S. (Eds.), *Investigations in the Triassic Chinle Formation*. Flagstaff, Arizona: Museum of Northern Arizona Bulletin 47, 1972.

Chronic, Halka. *Roadside Geology of Arizona*. Missoula, Montana: Mountain Press Publishing Co., 1983.

### LIFE OF AN ANCIENT LANDSCAPE

Ash, Sidney R., "Plant Megafossils of the Chinle Formation," *Investigations in the Triassic Chinle Formation*, by William J. Breed and Carol S. Breed. Flagstaff, Arizona: Museum of Northern Arizona, Bulletin 47, 1972.

Colbert, Edwin H. and Johnson, R. Roy, (Eds.), *The Petrified Forest Through the Ages, 75th Anniversary Symposium*. Flagstaff, Arizona: Museum of Northern Arizona, Bulletin 54, 1985.

Daugherty, Lyman H., *The Upper Triassic flora of Arizona*. Washington, D.C.: Carnegie Institution, Publication 526, 1941.

Long, Robert and Houk, Rose, *Dawn of the Age of Dinosaurs: The Triassic in Petrified Forest*. Petrified Forest, Arizona: Petrified Forest Museum Association, 1988.

Tidwell, William D., *Common fossil plants of Western North America, 2nd Edition*. Washington, D.C.: Smithsonian Institution Press, 1998.

### HUMANS IN THE PETRIFIED FOREST

Burton, Jeffery F., *Archeological Investigations at Puerco Ruin, Petrified Forest National Park, Arizona*. Tucson, Arizona: Western Archeological and Conservation Center, National Park Service, Publications in Anthropology No. 54, 1990.

Jones, Anne Trinkle, *Stalking the Past: Prehistory at Petrified Forest*. Petrified Forest, Arizona: Petrified Forest Museum Association, 1993.

Lister, Robert H. and Lister, Florence C., *Those Who Came Before: Southwestern Archeology in the National Park System*. Tucson, Arizona: Southwest Parks and Monuments Association, 1994.

McCreery, Patricia and Malotki, Ekkehart, *Tapamveni: The Rock Art Galleries of Petrified Forest and Beyond*. Petrified Forest, Arizona: Petrified Forest Museum Association, 1995.

Wendorf, Fred, with sections by Kate P. Kent, Earl H. Morris, and Ann O. Shepard. *Archaeological studies in the Petrified Forest National Monument*. Flagstaff, Arizona: Museum of Northern Arizona, Bulletin 27, 1953.

### PETRIFIED FOREST TODAY

Brown, D. E., *Biotic Communities, Southwestern United States and Northwestern Mexico*. Salt Lake City, Utah: University of Utah Press, 1994.

Leake, Dorothy Van Dyke, *Desert and Mountain Plants of the Southwest*. Norman, Oklahoma: University of Oklahoma Press, 1993.

Lowe, C. H., (Ed.), *The vertebrates of Arizona: landscapes and habitats, fishes, amphibians and reptiles, birds, mammals*. Tucson, Arizona: University of Arizona Press, 1967.

### EXPLORATION AND DEVELOPMENT

Ash, Sidney R., "The Search for Plant Fossils in the Chinle Formation," *Investigations in the Triassic Chinle Formation*, by William J. Breed and Carol S. Breed. Flagstaff, Arizona: Museum of Northern Arizona, Bulletin 47, 1972.

Foreman, Grant, (Ed.), *A Pathfinder in the Southwest: The Itinerary of Lieutenant A. W. Whipple during his Exploration for a Railroad Route from Fort Smith to Los Angeles in the Years 1853 and 1854*. Norman, Oklahoma: University of Oklahoma Press, 1941.

Lubrick, George M., *Petrified Forest National Park: A Wilderness Bound in Time*. Tucson, Arizona: University of Arizona Press, 1996.

Möllhausen, Baldwin, *Diary of a journey from the Mississippi to the coasts of the Pacific*. New York, New York, Johnson Reprint Corporation, 1969.

Ward, Lester H., *The Petrified Forest of Arizona*. Annual Report of the Smithsonian Institution for 1889, 1901.

## Acknowledgements

Petrified Forest Museum Association would like to offer special thanks to the PFMA Board of Directors for their support and oversight; Dr. Sidney Ash for his invaluable guidance and direction; T. Scott Williams for his energy and contributions; the Petrified Forest National Park Staff for their review and assistance; Joshua Wenger, Operations Manager, for his contributions and review; Bill Parker for his technical review and assistance; and Northland Publishing, Brian Billideau, John Pavich, David Jenney, and Tammy Gales-Biber for their help in making this project come together and for being a pleasure to work with—this is a partnership PFMA is certainly proud to have. Finally, a big thank you to all those not mentioned, who provided valuable assistance and moral support.

## All about Petrified Forest Museum Association

The Petrified Forest Museum Association is a nonprofit organization dedicated to the support of Petrified Forest National Park through a program of visitor services, publications, and other activities. The association was founded in December, 1941. From membership fees, donations, and the publication and sale of appropriate literature and interpretative items, the association currently provides over $190,000 annually to the park's informational, educational, and interpretative programs.

*For more information about the association, please contact us at:*
Petrified Forest Museum Association
Park Road 1, P.O. Box 2277
Petrified Forest, AZ 86028
(928) 524-6228
(928) 524-1509 fax
pfma@frontiernet.net

*To Contact the Park:*
Superintendent
Petrified Forest National Park
P.O. Box 2217
Petrified Forest, AZ 86028
(928) 524-6228
(928) 524-3567 fax
www.nps.gov/pefo